New Letters

A Continuation of *The University Review*

Some Writers We Have Published in Our First 86 Years:

W0038663

Diego Rivera
E.E. Cummings
J.D. Salinger
Pearl S. Buck
William Carlos Williams
James T. Farrell
Gwendolyn Brooks
Margaret Walker
Thomas Berger
Amiri Baraka
John Updike
Melvin B. Tolson
Chinua Achebe
Jack Gilbert
Kenneth Rexroth
Galway Kinnell
Mark Strand
Raymond Carver
Thomas Hart Benton
May Swenson
Marianne Moore
Edgar Lee Masters
Vance Randolph
Richard Wright
William S. Burroughs
Etheridge Knight
William Stafford
Kofi Awoonor
David Ignatow
Maxine Kumin
Allen Ginsberg
Sara Teasdale
A.D. Hope
Wilson Harris

NEW LETTERS

Subscribe online and find complete information
on awards for writers, workshops, audio archives and more:
www.newletters.org

New Letters (ISSN 0146-4930) is published quarterly by the University of Missouri-Kansas City. Subscriptions for individuals are: 1 year $28; 2 years $40; 5 years $75. Library Rates are: 1 year $36; 2 years $58; 5 years $114. Outside the U.S., add a $20 foreign surcharge per year. *New Letters on the Air* programs can be ordered for $3.99 for each audio download, or $7.99 each for a CD. See our catalogue and index at www.newletters.org. Donations can be tax deductions.

Address communications to: The Editor, *New Letters*, University of Missouri-Kansas City, 5101 Rockhill Road, Kansas City, MO 64110. Opinions expressed in *New Letters* are not necessarily those of the editor or of the University. Periodicals postage paid at Hanover, Pennsylvania.

New Letters is typeset in 11 point Leawood for body text, with CG Omega heads, and printed on 60-pound recycled, acid-free Cougar paper by The Sheridan Press, Hanover, Pennsylvania.

INDEXED in *Abstracts of English Studies, Humanities International Complete, Arts and Humanities Citation Index, Current Contents, Index to Book Reviews in the Humanities, Periodicals Contents Index.*

POSTMASTER: Changes of address should be sent to *New Letters*, University of Missouri-Kansas City, 5101 Rockhill Road, Kansas City, MO 64110.

Manuscripts in hard copy submitted to *New Letters* must be original typescript or clear photocopies, and will be returned only if a stamped, self-addressed envelope is provided. Or, see our online Submittable page. Manuscripts received between June 1 and August 1 will be returned unread.

Financial assistance for *New Letters* and *New Letters on the Air* is provided by the Missouri Arts Council, a state agency, by Patricia Cleary Miller, Ph.D., and the Miller-Mellor Association.

New Letters   (ISSN 0146-4930)

New Letters

Editor
Robert Stewart

Assistant Editor
Ashley Wann

Associate Editor
Christie Hodgen

NEW LETTERS ON THE AIR

Producer & Host   Assistant Producer
Angela Elam   Jamie Walsh

BKMK PRESS

Managing Editor   Assistant Managing Editor
Ben Furnish   Cynthia Beard

Student Staff
Kelsey Beck   Harmony Lassen
Sarah Chapman   Henry Shi

Advisory Editors
Catherine Browder   Denise Low

Awards Editorial Advisors
Catherine Browder   Ben Furnish   R.M. Kinder
Denise Low   Max McBride   John Moessner
Robert Oldshue   Steve Paul   Michael Pritchett   Kevin Rabas
Trish Reeves   Linda Rodriguez   Lisa D. Stewart

Past *New Letters* Editors
Clarence Decker   Alexander Cappon
David Ray   James McKinley

Cover design: Cynthia Beard

New Letters

A Continuation of *The University Review*
Published by the University of Missouri-Kansas City

ESSAY

REVIEWS & COMMENTARIES

ART GALLERY

THE *NEW LETTERS* MAGAZINE
READERS' AWARDS

READERS' FAVORITES FOR VOL. 85, 2018-2019

READERS' AWARD FOR FICTION

"The Game," by Gary Gildner

READERS' AWARD FOR POETRY

"The Opium Pillow," by John Balaban

READERS' AWARD FOR THE ESSAY

"Breathe," by J. Malcolm Garcia

HONORABLE MENTIONS

In Fiction: "Wind Phone," Catherine Browder.
In Poetry: "One Scorpio Night," Willis Barnstone.
In the Essay: "The Burning Door," Dennis Finnell.

OTHER WRITERS DISTINGUISHED BY OUR READERS

Michael Waters, Sergio Troncoso, Albert Goldbarth,
Roy Bentley, David Thoreen, Margot Livesey, Patricia Clark,
Jack Anderson, Dion O'Reilly, Margo Berdeshevsky, Trish Reeves.

*Save this and future issues of volume 86 and nominate your favorite
writing upon publication of our summer 2020 issue.*

That's It

An Editor's note

When the Japanese poet Basho lay dying, friends asked him to compose a death poem. According to scholar R.H. Blyth, Basho replied, "It has been customary to leave behind a death poem . . . but every moment of life is the last, every poem a death poem. Why, then, at this time, should I write one? In these my last hours, I have no poem."

Basho's principle, in its unnerving simplicity, its mystery, has come clear to me only now, decades since first reading that story. After more than 40 years of working on this magazine, as managing editor and then as editor, I realize that our goal with each publication was to create the final issue. Indeed, those editions of the magazine that I considered to be among the best were the hardest to live with. They would leave me terrified to do it over again. I often held a new edition in my hands, shortly after it came out, and would tell myself, That's it. I would never top it. Then, in a short time, we would start again to gather the new work of writers and artists. This process will continue under my successor, Christie Hodgen, a superb writer, herself.

What a privilege to work each day in a world in which every moment of life is the last. I did nothing to earn the intensity and power these editions have woken in me. I must be honest: The writing and art were gifts of genius and faith others have provided. Yes, in my first week as editor-in-chief, in 2002, I did pick up the phone and call one of my heroes, Brian Doyle, and, yes, he did immediately send an essay about the jazz masters Paul Desmond and Dave Brubeck, an amazing example of journalistic style and elegance.

I did reach out. I have passed to my student editors the advice of one of my predecessors and mentors, David Ray, who told me, "Editors don't just sit back and open the mail." Get out on the

street, I often said to aspiring editors. Be aggressive; and, yes,
I was the guy standing by to shake hands with the likes of Jim
Harrison, Grace Paley, Carolyn Kizer, Gwendolyn Brooks. An
editor can't will great work to come to his or her magazine, but,
as with the great poets, themselves, editors need to be present
for it.

Part of the mythology of editing involves the discovery of
unknown yet great writers, but, I must say, I felt that same thrill
of discovery when the well-known writer Janet Burroway, for
example, sent me her stories published here, or her many essays
we have published in the past. When the prominent essayist
Edward Hoagland sent me "In Africa," or "Hippies and Beats,"
I was shaken, again, to be in the presence of the never-before-
seen. I could not wait to get them into the magazine. How
fortunate to be awakened like that. Just the other day, I picked
up last summer's issue and reread a poem by Dion O'Reilly
called "Gorge," a leaping, gutsy, visceral, demanding poem I
never could have anticipated coming to us, and all I could think
of after reading it was, "I got to publish that."

—Robert Stewart

New Letters

WELCOMES

VICTORIA CHANG

SPRING 2020 COCKEFAIR CHAIR
WRITER-IN-RESIDENCE

University of Missouri-Kansas City
Tuesday, March 31, 2020.

Victoria Chang is the author of five poetry collections, most recently *Obit* (Copper Canyon, 2020), *Barbie Chang* (Copper Canyon, 2017), and *The Boss* (McSweeney's, 2013). She is the recipient of numerous awards including a Guggenheim Fellowship, a MacDowell Fellowship, a Poetry Society of America Alice Fay di Castagnola Award, and a Lannan Residency Fellowship. She helps run Antioch University's low-residency M.F.A. program, co-cordinates the Idyllwild Writers Week, and serves on the National Book Critics Circle Board. She lives in Los Angeles, California.

SELECTED EVENTS WILL INCLUDE:

- Discussion on Writing & Master Class
- Public Reading & Interview

Both open to the public: See our calendar of literary events at *www.newletters.org*.

Administered by the English department's Master of Fine Arts Program in Creative Writing and Media Arts, University of Missouri-Kansas City, College of Arts and Sciences, with financial support from the Cockefair Chair in Continuing Education.

University of Missouri-Kansas City, Department of English, 106 Cockefair Hall, 5121 Rockhill Road, Kansas City, Mo. 64110, (816) 235-1305. www.newletters.org.

STORE WINDOW.
PHOTOGRAPH BY REBECCA OFIESH.

Three Poems

TRISH REEVES

The Estate of Christian Jüengling, 1758

Among a coffy mill, a tee kittle, a knife, fork &
box, peuter basen, cup & 3 plates, 2 cheers, a table,
a chest, an iron stove and piece of Bees wax
are three books. The inventory is 25 lines long,
some lines include several entries as in:
a box ledd and sisirs, or four glasses
& some cups. The appraised value
comes to 58 Lb, 10 S, and 7 D.
Judged most valuable, in descending order:
Bills and bonds, Cash,
bed bedding & Bedsted,
waring apperil, the iron stove,
and the three books.
None of the other items are
worth a pound. Yet what I'd like
to ask is, What were you reading?
What did you find in a book
of enough interest to invest in?
Given your Christian name, as the phrase goes,
and my reading on such matters, I must guess
without hesitation that the Bible rested on the
chest. And then—considering you signed
your will in German script—I don't know—
the names that come to mind, Goethe, Kant,
Schiller come too late, and perhaps you were
more practical and somehow found a German-
English dictionary. I do not know, and have
come to an age of knowing some of what is
and is not of importance, so although I see
only two cheers in your inventory, I must say,
Three cheers for three books, Grandfather.

Holding the Edge

The lighthouse keeper's assistant, a severe sixty
feet below, rounded rock of granite in his fist,
beats the bell whose clapper never shipped,
and with ships still sailing toward the point,
though the fog soft, no lamp through a lens
will penetrate tonight
past the edge upon which the lighthouse
keeper sits and smokes, and, watching the fog,
polishes the lens far above the man
who, rock in hand,
so speaks
for the light.

The Night Clock

Years after the Pope found he couldn't sleep
(I do not posit it had to do with his prior position
as Inquisitor of Malta), this Fabio Chigi, in 1655,
asked the Campani brothers to make him one
of those clocks you may have wanted after 9/11—
or 11/8—something that wouldn't wake you in the night
with its illumination, yet if you glanced its way
you would see the correct numeral, as the wandering-
hour dial displayed 2 or 3 a.m. in a cut-out
by the glow of the oil lamp now inside the clock case;
only enough light to let you know that you remain
alive, though in a time that men more powerful than you,
you tell yourself, had set ticking, with no silent crank
encasement, no flue to channel the smoke
as farther and harder the brass tooth
drops and the gear train advances forward.

Three Poems

G E R A L D   S T E R N

Dreams

Deborah was waiting for me
at the landing in Boston
with the very young Stevie
her face purple, her neck broken,
and she was full of apology
for leaving the world that way
and she couldn't wait to tell me
she was following her dear one again on Visa,
more brazen this time than ever;

and I was carrying *The New Yorker*
that contained Susan Sontag's article
on Antonin Artaud
which I read on the ferry at an inside table
and I started immediately on it
though I was explaining my piece on Gil Orlovitz
who died on a sidewalk in New York
in front of his apartment house;

and Deborah's hair was white and she slipped her arm
    through mine
smiling through her wrinkles
and she had traded in the bottles on her back porch
for the nickel and dime deposits
exactly as her mother had done
when she wanted a few days away from the nine children
and her husband the doctor who talked endlessly about
    the hospital
and the orchards full of apples mostly Cortland
he walked through every day to smell the blossoms,

and I couldn't for a long time remember
how she soothed me out of a painful anxiety attack
only I was coming out of a bus then
and we walked through the Village for over an hour
deliberately coming late to an appointment
we didn't want to keep
when she was maybe in her early forties
where we half criticized and half praised
those we loved and hated
and later that day we sat in my car
waiting for six o'clock when we would be legal

and it all took place in two kinds of time
depending on how you looked at it
though I always said I hated poems
that were based on dreams
but this was as vivid as it gets
with all the transformations and conversions
and most of all for the compressions and tone changes
wherever it came from, whatever it meant,
wherever I was going with it,
so little did I know,
though now it is one of my main memories
nor does the mourning ever stop.

Red Emma

Since no one under 50 remembers much of
Emma Goldman and Eugene Debs
except one or two here and there

or knows that May Day was created in Chicago
from the backs of trucks and rotting vegetables

and since Woodrow is finally shown to be a brown rat
which I have been singing about for decades now
I have to go back into my kitchen
to make amends to the self-existent light
for those who are buried
both alive and dead

—on my knees or otherwise—

in the year of the pink flamingo
who, after all, comes from Africa not Florida
and flourished in Egypt in the days of Philo,
never on the West Coast or east
Fort Myers or Fort Lauderdale
standing on one vermilious leg in front of
the cheap motels I slept and wrote in,
once or twice I loved in, youths ago,
true to the rotting vegetables
which I proved by carrying a bag full of dictionaries
and swimming trunks in the back seat of my car
even Berkman would have loved for its
static radio and its homemade paint job,
Oh, bless me Father Divine.

Beginning with Kate

Beginning with Kate, a ten-year-old golden retriever
sleeping all day and
tethered to a baby grand, choosing
the cold marble to lie down on instead
of the nearby commercial carpet in the
lobby of the Betsy,
a grand hotel at the northernmost end of Ocean
Drive in Miami Beach, city of Jackie Gleason
and Andrew Warhola, the latter of ghosts you might say
presiding over the annual Basel Schnazzel
where I, with a cane between my legs,
on the most comfortable chair in the whole lobby
keeping Kate company and poking her from
time to time to remind her of the good days
of pork unlimited surrounded by
fat galore and bone softened by cooking
for we were spoiled by loving owners
we couldn't repay enough by growling and barking
as they sat on their sofas doing their own
wondrous barking, the music we listened to
as we stretched out on their wood and wool and grass,
me too for I was a dog in those days
and sort of trotted like a tan horse
up and down the streets of my six rivers.

Okra

PETER BALAKIAN

My mother stewed you
with onions and tomatoes,

then rice and chicken stock
to simmer for hours,

so when I came in from the sandlot
with some bloodied arm or face

your steam was a counter play.
It took me awhile to savor

the slide of your slimy pods
down my throat—

your seeds rolled
the roof of my mouth—

the pods floated like caciques
in the broth.

I came to see your hieroglyphics
in red clay

because Black women sizzled you up
in the big house

to rebut the theft,
to smuggle in

canoes of the Niger—
dug-out tree trunks,

pirogues of the heart,
rushing water

roux of gumbo:
ok u ru in Igbo—

words on the roof of my mouth—
anagrams in broth.

SPRING FIELD ROAD, OIL ON CANVAS,
BY CAROL ZASTOUPIL.

Two Excerpts from a Novel

JANET BURROWAY

Lady Lazarus, Cambridge, England, 1956

There was nobody on the High Street. At least, nobody until he turned into the lodge and that Weedy Wanker of a porter said, "Terrible, isn't it, sir? But that's fen weather for you." And handed him two square envelopes—overblown Christmas cards from the aunts, no doubt—and a notice about the Atheists Club.

The granite steps to his digs were ice. Worn like ice blocks shaved in the middle—where had he seen that? There hadn't been a gas fire lit in the whole college since break began. There were crystals edging all his window panes and a cobweb outside lined in hoarfrost. He'd saved up eight shilling coins and stuck five of them in the meter, then turned on both the waffle grate under the mantel and the gas ring in the gyp room. There was a tin of spaghetti sauce, a half bag of fettuccine and several damp, possibly mouse-nibbled Hobnobs. He sat by the fire in his overcoat, not wanting to go out again but wanting a meal at least. Lyons would be closed, but maybe the chow mein place on Magdalene.

Down the steps again, thinking again of the very thing he wanted out of his mind, Blunt Bastard whom he was biologically obliged to call his father: *And where was the sauce for the veg?* Then Mouse Mum: *There was no sauce to this, it was brussel sprouts, meant to be eaten plain.* And Blunt: *Well, it* tastes *bloody plain.* The mouse defense, the bastard rant, his own rebuttal rant, the tears, the bloody frigging *inconsequence* of it all. Thinking of that. So it brought him up short when he turned under the back arch and saw her on Clare Bridge.

She was leaning on the balustrade over the murk, long body propped against the stone ball that had suffered a major gouging at some point in its seven hundred year history. Flat shoes too thin for the weather: a Scholarship Girl. Wearing her gown over her dark coat, although the proctors wouldn't be out until term started: a Good Girl, then. Closer, he saw she was aiming a little box Kodak at—what?—nothing to take a picture of, the green water lapping at the pier. He remembered that when she took pictures for the Amateur Dramatic Club, she didn't pose people in their costumes but snapped them backstage in their skivvies, or in the wings in all kinds of undignified poses no use for the programme. Simone something; he couldn't remember her last name.

So he said, "Simone the Beauvoir," and she turned, a lit smile in the middle of a pallid face.

"Hullo, Jamie."

"What are you doing here?"

"I was thinking what it would be like to jump in. It looks like lentil soup."

"Suicidal, are you?"

"I don't know. I don't have much experience with it."

"No, I meant, what are you doing back? Didn't you go away for vac?"

"I went to Helene's for Christmas. Which was nice of them, but . . . "

"Posh."

She gave a shrug, of the mouth only. Something else working in her eyes. Depressed for real, maybe?

She said, "And I had work to do, you know. You went home?"

"Mmm."

"That was posh as well."

"Oh, no. We're nouveau, barely ascended to the local council." He saw his father stretching his wattles as he tucked his napkin.

She lifted an eyebrow. "Why are *you* back early?"

"You know: work to do."

The politic thing was to ask her along to the Chinese place. But if he suggested it, he might be required to pay for her, and he had to rein in. He could foresee all the dreary problems he'd face this term for having rejected the Bastard's begrudging pocket money—though it had felt good, seeing the usual allowance in that outstretched hand, to have turned on his heel and left the house.

"Look, I've got some spaghetti and a jar of sauce upstairs. And some plonk, I think. Why don't we put on the kettle and share it?"

He'd chatted her up at Andy's once, to no particular purpose. She had eyes and a smile, but no breasts; her gown flowed straight from her shoulders. And she was wary now. Wary Mary the Scholarship Girl, looking again into the lentil soup of the Cam in winter.

"No strings," he said.

*   *   *

Still, she seemed willing. Between them they scraped the cast-iron pan and he opened a second bottle of red. He was glad he'd bought a case last term when he was flush. She plunked down beside him on the tatty carpet in front of the couch. She laughed at his jokes, and even when he called his mother Franny Fogwhistle. She volunteered that things had been awkward at Helene's too, the formality of every ritual gesture and dance of gratitude. So he offered his theory of language *a la* Hobbes: language as Social Contract; you never know if what you mean by a word is what I mean by it, so every conversation is a ragbag of approximations.

"Hobbes, eh?" she said.

"I'm very taken with Hobbes at the moment."

"'Nasty, brutish and short,'" she offered.

"Nasty British shit, the lads say."

"You're Philosophy, Politics and Economics."

"PPE. Or PEE, as the lads have it."

"Was that a good choice for you?"

Oddly personal thing to ask, that. She was an odd girl. "Why do you ask?"

"Well, you seem very keen at the ADC."

"Amateur dramatics is my sport. PPE is supposed to prepare me for real life."

"And does it?"

He was a tad unnerved by her concentration, the solemnity of it, though it might be a good sign. Their meal's debris sat on the carpet in front of them. He pushed it aside, laid a forearm along the couch cushions behind her back and cupped a hand at her shoulder. "I'm fine with the philosophy and politics, but I'm buggered if I get the math. I'll get a second class degree and be stuck in my father's shop for the next millennium, hawking Gentlemen's Bespoke." He said this lightly, and despaired.

She turned toward him, suddenly arch. Flirting? "There's a certain nobility in cloth, though. Think of the centuries of artists painting robes and their flowing folds!"

He said, "Thank you, Aldous Huxley," and she laughed. So far so good. He nuzzled at her neck and took little nibbling bites with his lips only, just as his brother Trevor had told him about back in Ealing when he was too young to hear it and went, "Eeeuw." But it had stuck in his mind, and it had stood him in good stead before this. Now the muscles along her neck seemed to shiver, and she stretched her jaw aloft. Inviting his mouth?

"I'm swotting up for a scholarship to America," she said. "If *I* get a second, I'll end up in some polytechnic in South London, teaching the Wombles their own canon."

Her mood was slippery, serious to flip. They broke the Hobnobs in shards and downed each with a swallow of the cheap red. She stretched in a limber, unself-conscious way. Provocative? She said Arden House had emptied out for the holiday, and that only the British would think of stuffing all the foreigners together in one digs, and that she liked Amrita the Pakistani and Maria Leina the Spaniard but not Nadila the Turk; and that the most un-English student in Arden House was Dodie the American, who went off for holiday to Paris and Vence—"Vence, not Venice"—in a checkerboard skirt and a red bandeau with a Samsonite overnighter.

He pictured Dodie, lanky and full of herself, fashion model, author of lush and in his view overwritten poetry, sought after for a date or a bash-up. Envious girls were always ready to discuss her vulgarity.

But Simone's tone was admiring. "Dodie's not trying out this term for the ADC. She says she has to devote herself to her writing."

He asked if she herself hadn't wanted to go home for Christmas, but she shrugged and ducked her head, not answering. She said instead, "I have this phantom in my mind, somebody who is me and not-me, going about her business in Liege, wearing a cloth coat bald at the pockets, with a hairnet and a flat hat. But if I were there now, this is not the way I would look. It's the way twenty-five-year-olds looked when I *was* there, before. Now no such creature would exist."

He felt a great wave of pity for her. He remembered that she'd been a refugee. He made his voice low and asked if her parents had died in the war. She said, "Oh. What does a temporal label illuminate? We say: *In the war, in the morning, in the seventeenth century.* What does that explain?" She was an odd girl. He kissed her in what he hoped was a soulful manner—she let him—and slipped his hand down to her rib cage. She smelled of bread.

His shillings were gone now, and she'd contributed just one. He'd turned the fire to low; the chill was spreading. He reached up over the sofa, dragged the blanket off the back and tucked it onto the carpet below her hip. She huddled under.

Her head waggled and she suddenly began to slur. "'R' you trying out for *Troilus and Creshida*?"

"No, I'll stage manage; stick to what I'm good at."

"I thought you'd audition for Thershites." And then—showing off her Thersites voice—"*. . . how if he had boilsh, full, all over, generally? . . . And those boilsh did run?*" Immediately she reddened, her cheeks so hot he could see it in the dim light of the fire. "I di'n't mean. . . . " Well, he had acne pits. So what? She had a spider nevus on her cheekbone, a little mesh of breakages in the porcelain. She rushed on, "I'll have a go at Cashandra, but of coursh Victoria will get it, and I'll be fobbed off with taking the pho-tos."

That was probably true. "There's a certain nobility in camera work, though," he said. "The play must close; the pictures are forever."

She said, "Thank you, Mr. Gielgud," and they both giggled.

"But. Apart from Cassandra and America, what do you want?" He waited for her to say what girls always said, even the smart ones, even the Scholarship Girls: *a home and family, a good husband.*

She said, "Shtiletto heels and a set of Samshonite."

He guffawed and toasted her for a good sport and emptied the bottle into her glass. St. Mary's chime had sounded ten and the porter would close the gates up early, it being vac. There was nobody to disturb them but all the same he felt exposed if he didn't shut the outer door. He got up carefully, unsteadier than he'd thought. He didn't know if she understood the closed oak would be a signal that he was either studying or snogging and was not to be disturbed. Gingerly still he opened the baize door a crack, reached out and closed the oak, closed the baize again.

Now she was blanket-wrapped, head lolling back on the sofa, cooing softly. "Ceiling going 'round. T' mush plonk." He inserted himself under the cover and shifted her head back onto a pillow on the floor. She put her arms around him and hiccupped a little. "Woo-oo!" she said, enigmatically. He hadn't managed this all that many times: his zip, her garter belt, the blanket tangle, her plucking at his fingers and moaning, "Sloo-ow . . . " But he was glad to be hard, and when she started pushing his chest away with some force, his anger excited him. "Slower!" He found the elastic of her knickers and stuck two fingers up into her, which she was supposed to like, instead of which she bucked and the cushion slid, her head bouncing on the floor. She said, "No!" and he said, "Your mouth says no but your eyes say yes," which Trevor had told him always worked. It didn't. She said, "Can't. Can't" or "Cant. Cant," or was it (his mind flailing), "Kant, Kant." She shoved him sideways and again his anger aroused him so he pulled at her knickers and had them down with one hand, the other pinning her forearm on the floor while with her free hand she battered at him, scratched his collar bone above his vest, drew blood.

A memory came unbidden out of his childhood: a pond somewhere; he sat in the prow of a boat while Bastard stood midships pulling at Mouse Mum, trying to get her to step in; but she reared back and pummeled him with her forearms, which made the boat wash away from the dock, and Bastard, holding tight to her shoulders, pulled her into the widening water. She landed with cartwheeling arms, face first, rising drenched and fuming in soak no higher than her thighs; a comedy. He had been in the prow, but he always saw this from his father's perspective, having heard it retold so often. "Dined out on it," Bastard said of the hilarious anecdote.

This image was no use to him. He thrust it out of mind and managed to get his free hand under her jumper, clutched at her boob—surprisingly soft after all—and latched onto the first film scene that came: a Yank soldier, bare chest under an ammo belt, comes out of the palm trees toward a girl hanging laundry. She's wearing a wrapped skirt and a bikini top (Who knows why? Never mind that). Her tits are lifted by the top, pressed together and bulging over a little bit of some edging on the bra. The soldier comes up to her and she turns, sloe-eyed, wanting it.

"Stop. Stop now!" Simone rocked her hips side to side so he couldn't manage to get in. His anger intensified and intense was good, good and then urgent, urgent and then unstoppable. Between pinning her arm and fending off her flailing other hand he couldn't get inside her. So he pressed his member against her belly in the hollow formed by her hip bone, pushed once and came. Needed. Huge.

He collapsed on her, and she too went limp except for her thrashing head. She made a guttural sound. But he felt okay about it. She wouldn't get pregnant, or be able to say she did.

He went for a towel in the gyp room and wiped her and then the rug. She was still now, hand over her eyes, but when he went to pull her knickers up she said, "Don't touch me!"

Oh, for Christ's sweet sake. She wasn't going to go all Victorian on him now, was she? These cunts.

"Stay away from me!"

Nevertheless, he was a gentleman. "Look. Come on to bed," he said. "The gates are closed, and there's no way you can climb the wall. You can get a night's sleep and make it back to Arden House before they miss you in the morning."

She rolled into the counterpane, away from him. "Come on," he said. But she stayed wrapped up there, spitting something inaudible, then lying ostentatiously quiet, quiet as the dead; so he got in his bed in the recess and pulled the curtain.

But once in bed his anger—a sense of being wronged compounded with a sense of having somehow failed, of being wrongly blamed for having failed—took some large-mammal form and had him by the teeth, morphed into his bastard father and back to Hobbes, *nasty British shit* which was not now amusing, back and forth between the unfairness and his father and Hobbes and back again. How dare she? Get him hot and then act as if he'd violated her unlikely bloody virginity. When he didn't even put it in! It was not as if she was any great prize that a fellow would swank about in the showers. The starch-stiff sheet rasped and twisted against his legs. He would be ragged tomorrow for lack of sleep.

When he woke she was already gone.

He put it out of mind. Why should he care? But the rage sat dull at the center of his forehead; the lines in his phil books blurred as if he had a hangover. Bitch. Blue-baller. She knew the rules. She'd been with him right up to the last minute, egging him on with her stretching and kissing and all that "slo-o-ow" stuff they all do that everybody knows they think they have to because of church or sacred womanhood or some crap. Then made as if he'd forced himself on her. The twat. Screw the lot of them.

He didn't run into her, there's a blessing, not at the Mill nor on the High Street, not even at the Atheists Club meeting, where he'd planned to cut her dead.

But January fourteenth, a Saturday, he went along to the ADC tryouts as scheduled, where the bike rack was crowded and the air crackling with ambition. The girls sat in the shabby front row theater seats, pulling on their skirts and making interested faces, fourteen of them to read for four parts—which was the opposite of the social scene, since there were fifteen men for every girl at Cambridge and the dollies usually had their pick. She was there, all right, head down, book on her lap, twisting at her hair.

This morning was for the girls. The men would scramble another day, but, Shakespeare plays being replete with male parts, they would all be cast. He was in charge of passing out the audition info and calling the hopefuls up by turn. She sat at the far end near the door, accepting the page without lifting her head. Simone *Lerrante*, it said on the roster. Right and good. Halfway through the alphabet, so by the time they got to her she'd understand she could expect no special treatment. Geoffrey St. John handed round the scripts, which caused Miss Simone Linear to lift her own dog-eared Penguin paperback, showing off. Oh, and then, of course, she gave Geoffrey that doe-eyed limpid look, that panting-dogface of the Sin-jin Fan Club—doesn't everybody love a pretty boy, though?—whereas it was no secret Geoff was lusting after Dodie the Yank Wonder Woman and her red bandeau. And was probably secretly gay underneath it all.

They went through the first four Cassandras at a leisurely pace, Geoffrey letting each of them try it again with "a touch more urgency," "*Cry, Trojans, cry! Lend me ten thousand eyes / And I will fill them with prophetic tears*" and "*Look how thou diest! Look how thy eye turns pale! / Look how thy wounds do bleed at many vents!*"

"*Die-est,*" Geoffrey said. "Dra-a-aw out the syllables so we feel the weight of the dying." His forelock *would* flop in his face. He should chop it off but it was his gambit just to shove it back as if it surprised him every time. To the next wannabe he said, "You must *see* it. You're a see-er. We must *see you seeing it.*"

After that the pace picked up a bit, which was standard. You get to know at once who's in contention; after the first few lines, the first five feet. Also you get bored. You couldn't spend half an hour with every one of the fourteen. "*Look how thou diest! Look how thy eye turns pale! Look how thy wounds do bleed at many vents!*"

It was after lunch break before Simone came up, and by then you could see she was ragged with nerves. She got up on stage not by going back round the wobbly steps but by sitting at the proscenium edge, swinging her legs over and pushing up on hands and knees.

She moved well, he had to give her that. She had presence; you knew it when she took the stage. And her voice was clear, and carried. All the same. He could have told her exactly what was wrong with her audition. What was wrong was being an immigrant, if you didn't mind his saying so. A ruddy foreigner. She read Cassandra as if she learned Shakespeare from the movies. *"Look how thou diest! Look how thy eye turns pale!"* She cocked her elbows. She spread her legs. She read Cassandra as if she was Barbara Stanwyck, Melodrama Mama in shoulder pads and a canted hip. Whereas the English girls had got it in their bones. They read the rhythm of the line against the rhythm of the sense, so you got both natural speech and natural poetry. The whole time Simone was reading—reciting, rather, for like an overeager novice she had it all by heart—she never turned in his direction. She focused here and there, down front, to the back of the house, at every chance toward Geoffrey. But in those invisible intersecting arcs she never came within a yard of catching his eye.

There were five more to read, and then Victoria last, a fortunate accident of the alphabet, since it would have been clear to a blind man that she was the one. A short, stolid girl, fierce-faced in spite of a nubby nose. The formidable intelligence of her!—with a man's ragged basso and the poise of Joan of Arc. Yes, Victoria won it fair and square, obvious to anyone with half a brain and there's an end to it. Geoffrey thanked them all and lied about the difficulty he would have in choosing, and said that if you were cast he would be in touch by Wednesday noon.

They filed out to the bike rack. He stationed himself at the door to take the audition info back, but she hung at the stage chatting to Geoffrey and Muriel, so he had to decide whether to wait for her or not. He stayed where he was, uncertain, until she finally came toward the exit. He put his hand out for the page. But halfway down the aisle she draped the sheet on the arm of a chair and— Muriel, Geoffrey, Victoria, all of them seeing this—veered deliberately off toward the side door, her head held high to make obvious the snub.

*   *   *

It wasn't clear when or how he got the idea, or even why. One minute he was certain she'd get her comeuppance in the casting, and the next there it was, fully thought out in his mind. It was during the discussion at the ADC, where Muriel was picked for Cressida and Victoria for Cassandra. Or it was in Hall when Rupert Forth turned over a forkful of spaghetti into the lumpy mash and said, "The purpose of mashed potatoes is to keep the noodles on your fork." Or it was at Ian and Thom's on Green Street up over the ironmonger's, booze in the kitchen and a groaning board: Scotch eggs and sausage rolls, six kinds of cheese, an urn full of Sharp's Creamy Toffee. Cool jazz on the gramophone. Ian served the best wine and food because he came from real money, old money, but he shared the house with Thom, a scholarship boy who had a cockney accent and looked like a ruddy butcher. Because both were Communists. *Workers unite* and all that. Nobody pointed out the contradiction between the politics and the French cheese.

The room got crowded and full of fug and the sour smell of breathed-out wine. The Leavisites squared off against the fans of Krook, and then somebody brought up the question of identity, post Sartre.

Ian said, "All your cells are changed out every seven years, so on the level of matter you are an entirely different person."

Thom said, "And on the level of politics, everything you believed seven years ago is bollocks."

Firth said, "People don't change. They can only be *redeemed*."

Ian said, "Even as I stand here, I am becoming someone other. Two minutes ago I was a creature who had never heard Firth propose redemption!"

No wonder, with a slow drip of drivel like that, he retreated into the wine, a Beaujolais his father would have made a great fuss over, and then a raffia-wrapped Chianti some tosser had brought. Drank so much of it that he drifted into Ian's room, lay on Ian's couch, the ceiling meandering a parabola over his head and his throat clamped, tossed back into a rage that seared his eyes.

It could not have been simpler. On Tuesday afternoon when he knew the Lit-Crit classes met, he called Arden House and asked for Simone Lerrante. Mrs. Guinea said she would take a message, so he asked her to write it down. Mr. Geoffrey St. John was pleased to invite Miss Simone Lerrante to accept the part of Cassandra in the upcoming ADC production of *Troilus and Cressida.* Her presence was requested at first reading Sunday the twenty-second at ten o'clock.

He forgot his manager's notes and had to cycle back, so he hurried through the black rectangle of the lobby to the auditorium and the stage, harsh under worklights that momentarily blinded him. They had drawn three study tables together, but they were mostly not seated yet. Clive was winding himself up in the dusty curtains. Geoffrey stood at the head with his director's notebook splayed, and Muriel and Keith pored over their lines, but most were sitting on the apron bumping their heels against the rise, or lounging in the seats whose velvet upholstery was pocked like divots on a golf green. A few waved or said hello. He counted the cast and saw that there were several missing; Geoffrey would be giving his oration about the sacred rules of promptness in the the-a-tah. Meanwhile he was placing copies of the rehearsal schedule from a pile of fluttery onionskin. He had trouble getting them to settle, and—fooling around for the front row—laid a hand on each with an admonitory or a conjuring gesture.

Then she was there, out of breath, blinking from the dark lobby, full of agitated joy. Oh, yes: she had made herself a new Dodie kind of skirt, flared and tweed instead of the mole-colored down-to-her-calves kind of thing she usually wore. She came into the orchestra pit and teetered there on her thin ballet flats. A few lifted a hand to her. But it felt wrong. It was unlikely she'd been asked to take pictures of first read-through. Everyone looked at her, waiting, with an air of general quizzicalness. Geoffrey was first to break toward her. One corner of his mouth creased deeper than the other. "Simone?"

"Hi," she said, still breathless. "Sorry I'm late. What a day to have a flat! I had to borrow someone's bike."

There was a hiatus, Geoffrey rolling up a sheet of onion skin. He took half a step. "Hullo, Simone. Can I do something for you?"

She shook her curls with a little laugh. "Is that the rehearsal schedule you have there?"

Victoria drew her face back into a double chin. Firth clapped her heels against the stage. Muriel's smart-chopped hair sat along her jaw like a scimitar. Geoffrey was tall and broad-shouldered but when he was unsure of himself he moved with an endearing sidle, as if he were clumsy once and had incorporated clumsiness as a part of style.

He said, tentative, "I'm afraid we have exactly as many as we need for the cast."

Sometimes you really can see someone thinking. See the process of realization as it unfolds. They were all looking at her now. Her cheeks were aflame. He thought he saw that spider nevus crawl. She picked up her shoulders in a fair approximation of a shrug. Pulled back the corners of her mouth and then let them fall.

Geoffrey went to her. Oh, he is kind! He held up the curl of onionskin like a torch. "Simone—I'm sorry if there's been some kind of misunderstanding."

She wavered, barely. Brightly widened those eyes. "No, no. I just thought," she said, "I thought I should just come along and let you know. That I won't be able to take the photos this production. I won't have time, you see. I have to, I have to, devote myself. To my studies."

And turned and ran.

The production was a success, the reviews good and the houses full. He felt reasonably secure in his place among them, this community, these creatures of doubleness, in fear of being singled out and frantic to be seen, in terror of the thing they most desired, warm-blooded puppets bonded in the glare. His was the mundane part, the anchoring keeper of times and places, seeing to ropes and boxes and bottles of diluted tea. It suited him.

But at the end of February, after *Troilus* closed and just when he ought to have started cramming toward the Tripos, he contracted the bugger of all colds. He huddled in his room in a pathological avoidance of his books. Days he lay on the threadbare sofa, evenings he got himself upright and dragged down to The Mill, where he drank till last call and took himself back into the smell of old sick and eucalyptus drops. One night he dreamed his head was forcibly tipped back and his nostrils plugged with a rubber-tipped bottle like those they used at school, his head poured full of mucilage that ran into his sinuses, his ear canal, between his skull and brain. In the dream he must lie very still or it would harden and glue his eyes in place. When he woke he told the words over in the dark: acedia, anhedonia, abulia, anomie: *spiritual torpor, a lack of the capacity to experience pleasure, the inability to make a decision, deep malaise.* He had the thought that definition was befriending, though why this should be so he couldn't say. And it did not get him to the books that would have given him the definitions his exams required.

April was a little better. His sinuses cleared and the crocuses came out on Clare College Backs. He began to hear the odd rumor here and there that Simone Lerrante

and Geoffrey St. John were an item. And then that she'd
been taken on for supervision in The English Philosophers
(*from Plato to Sartre*, the wags said) by Professor Daiches at
Jesus College—a rarity for a Newnham girl. Someone said
that American Dodie had disappeared at a magazine launch
with Leonard Hawk, and when they reappeared he had
bloody bite marks on his cheek. He himself had a couple
of successes, one with a Girton girl who was known to put
out, and one with another Newnhamite who invited him to
her row-house, where they had to suppress any noise on
account of the thinness of the walls.

One more odd thing. (Simone was an odd girl.) One
night at The Mill, John Wing told him he had seen her, after
that morning's Leavis lecture on *The Dubliners*, straddling
her bike on Mill Bridge and throwing her little box Kodak
into the Cam.

*   *   *

One day he had to deliver an ADC accounting of the
Troilus production to the sponsoring don, who had her
digs in Sedgewick Hall; and he spotted Dodie, brushing
the vestiges of snow from the shoulders of the bronze boy
with the dolphin on Sedgewick fountain. Dodie's nose
was swollen and her hair stringy with fever grease under
a babushka scarf. No off-to-Paris-with-a-Samsonite about
her now.

"We've both been ill, apparently," he said.

"D'you think? This rotten climate."

"You live at Arden House," he said, "like Simone
Lerrante." He had no idea he was going to say that, and no
idea why.

"Oh, Simone," said Dodie. "She's just got a Fulbright to
America, you know."

"No, I didn't know. Well, good for her. That's capital.
Brilliant, is she?"

"Bright enough for America anyway!" Dodie laughed, rather crudely he thought.

He said, "She's tight with Geoffrey St. John, I understand."

"Oh, nah, I think that's over. He wasn't going to move to America, and she wasn't moveable."

"Ah, right, she's strong-headed." He smiled in a way that he hoped conveyed that he knew a thing or two about the strong head of Simone Lerrante.

But Dodie said, "I don't know about strong-headed. She's just mad that her daddy died."

"In the war," he said, confused.

"I mean mad at him for dying." And she turned abruptly to the dolphin boy again.

Over the next few days he began to think that he had made assumptions for which he had no basis, and wondered if Simone wasn't possibly admirable and admired: Geoff. Daiches. Fulbright. Dodie. And quite suddenly he leaped ahead to something like remorse—for he didn't know, really, what she thought of him or what, from her point of view, had really gone wrong that night. He might have misunderstood her reactions, perhaps even hurt her by not calling on her afterward, by seeming to cut her in the street. Had he cut her in the street? He couldn't be sure if he had done so or only imagined it. He was sorry he'd made her spend the night on the couch and leave without so much as a cuppa. Why had she thrown her camera in the Cam (*Cam-camera*), in such a public way? Did she assume it would get back to him, or was she only getting rid of the extraneous, in favor of "devoting" herself to study?

And how had she and Geoffrey St. John got together? He could well imagine Geoffrey stopping Simone after lecture, just to say something consoling. He could see them going to Lyons for a coffee, Simone confiding about the trick, the two of them even figuring out who might have played it. But this did not make him feel "caught" or worried for his

reputation. Geoffrey had apparently found out for himself
what S.L. meant by "no." If he felt remorse, it was shot
through with slivers of pride that he had been led on and
dumped, like Geoff, by an apparently famous totty.

It was fortuitous (a word he did not mistake for
fortunate like some of the lads) that just that week he had
a letter from his Mum enclosing thirty pounds; a princely
sum, which she had probably scraped together out of the
grocery money. Her note said that he needn't mention it to
his father. No fear. He bought another case of plonk and a
wool scarf out of Eaden Lily. And, on impulse, a dozen red
roses not from the stalls in the market but from a proper
flower shop, half a crown a stem, to be delivered in a box to
Miss Simone Lerrante at Arden House on Barton Road. He
took a long time over the card, in which he did not want to
say anything directly apologetic or, God knows, to suggest
he wanted to take her out again. But something friendly,
something no-foul, one scholar to another. In the end he
wrote, "Congratulations on your Fulbright. Well done!" He
signed it "James" and let it go at that.

It was when he got back from The Mill just before curfew
that that Wanker of a Porter stopped him at the lodge.
"'Ere, sir, there's a package for you, dropped off personal
by a young lady on her bicycle. She'd've had a dicey time to
balance it."

The long box was still tied with its satin ribbon. He
carried it up the stone steps wondering if the shop had got
it wrong, if they had delivered it to his address instead of
hers. But he did not really think that. He thought she had
sent it back. Or, according to the porter, brought it back.
And it was no real surprise, when he'd fed the gas meter and
laid the box on the counter in the gyp room, to find inside
in their brittle green paper the dozen roses, each of their
heads chopped neatly just below the bud. Not chopped
either, but deliberately sliced; each limp head severed with
the precision of an X-acto knife.

Transit: District of Columbia—Columbia, Mo., 1964

They roll south and inland through the dark: Fredericksburg, Richmond, Charlottesville, Covington. It doesn't make immediate sense that they should begin by going south, but it has been explained to her that they must do so to pick up Highway 64, which will take them west. The Greyhound stops every couple of hours so people can trickle dimes into the Coke machines or sit at the counters to eat burgers or hot pot pies. Some disappear and others take their place, youths with duffles, women with whining children and their gear in shopping bags, businessmen in seersucker carrying scuffed brown satchels.

All summer she sat stunned in the Library of Congress waiting for her life to begin again, studying the way the light pooled on the base of the brass lamp, doing research on her cuticles. Now she has no more self than a fruit pit spat out over the Virginias. She is a traveling hodge-podge; she might as well have dressed out of Darla Moxham's old dress-up chest: a work shirt, her dirty hair concealed under a scarf knotted on her neck, schoolgirl flats, and a skirt in "permanent" pleats that have splayed under her and balloon out over her bottom when she stands. The bus hurtles through acres of Appalachian hardwood—poplar, maple, hickory—the road a tunnel in blue trees. At dawn the haze swags like organdy among the branches. They descend toward Lewisburg past billboards touting *Lost World Caverns.* They stop for slabs of ham with eggs and grits. Half-a-dozen passengers scatter into the empty alleys behind the station, and as many materialize to fill their still-warm seats. It is nine years since the first Freedom ride, and federal law has ended segregation, but the black passengers sit mostly at the back.

An exception: At Beckley, a teenaged boy gets on in a letter sweater (he will not remove it even in the rising heat), his Afro cropped and tended, his neck thicker than his handsome head, strangling a disreputable radio by its handle. He swivels left and right with a readiness for any challenge, then slings himself in the front seat across from the driver. *To everything (turn, turn, turn),* says the radio, *there is a season (turn, turn, turn).* In Huntington he helps a black girl with her luggage— she in a yellow sundress like a bell, her long legs as clapper. By the time they hit Kentucky the girl has moved across the aisle beside him. Her laughter rides above the radio and the hum of tires. *Blowin' in the wind.*

At Morehead they change drivers, taking on a rotund gnome who beams *how-do* at them and mops his bald head with a paper towel. At Owensville three elder ladies in pillbox hats, carrying each a small hard-sided suitcase, settle themselves with decorous laughter. At Mount Sterling a portly man boards who lifts the flap of his leather vest, removes a pistol from his belt and wraps it carefully in a shirt before stowing it on the shelf above.

Letter-sweater and the black belle are a couple now. They purr and murmur, the boy's mowed head bent toward her. *Kisses much sweeter than wine.* At Winchester a lumbering white giant picks his way to the back, mumbling and twitching in his plaid flannel. "Simmadun," he seems to murmur, "desiban at shee." The travelers consult each other with their eyes: *Did anybody understand him?* Simone tries to read, but lack of sleep has settled as a grainy film on her eyes. The muscles of her back are knotted.

Hills shallower, trees more sparse, the landscape spreads itself under a sun so fierce that the air conditioning concedes defeat, and damp is trapped under Simone's shirt like a layer of long underwear. At Shelbyville they pull into a truck stop behind half-a-dozen eighteen-wheelers and spill out into a little cumulus of diesel fuel and gnats.

The café is a long stucco rectangle with, inside, two separate soda fountains that Simone takes for a sign of recent desegregation. The place is already aclatter with lunch, the walls decked with paper hydrangeas and photographs of baseball teams. The smell of hot fat disinclines her, so she takes a table by the window and, nevertheless determined to go local, orders a Coke and a moon pie. While she eats, she stares at the laminated map tacked to the window frame, which, although they are in Indiana, bears the logo *You Have Entered the Deep South*. Depth is represented as a cliff along the Mason-Dixon line. She feels the drop-off in her stomach.

There's a commotion beyond the counter at the far end of the café, a scraping of chairs and a thin yelp, and Simone looks up to see the white giant, his massive jaw squatting in his plaid shirt collar, fling a chair at a plate glass window. It's a plastic scoop-molded kind of chair that bounces and clatters across the linoleum. Nevertheless passengers back or sprint toward the door while the man roars something garbled, "stuck the nongs," or "stuggernogs." Even at this distance Simone, half out of her chair too, can see his spit fly. It's impossible to tell whether the rage is directed at anyone in particular. The cashier is shouting into the telephone.

The passengers fan out under the fuel-pump awning, embarrassed by their fear.

"Is he crazy?"

"What was he saying?"

"I don't know. I think a coupla truckers got him down."

The passengers find their bus, fueled and parked alongside the pumps, and climb aboard shaking their heads at each other, made a community by what they've seen. On the bus they grin, sheepish. The paunchy man in the leather vest asks, "Was he on drugs, or what?" This is somehow the wrong question. The black boy turns up his radio. . . . *such a lot of world to see.*

"Was he one 'the truckers, or a local?"

"No, he was on the bus, before, there at the back."

"Was he fightin *with* somebody?"

"They called the sheriff, though."

"Plain crazy, is what I'd say."

"Crazy, lord!"

At this angle they can't see into the café, and gradually the talk subsides. They wait, as they have waited at every so-called rest stop for eighteen hours now. Simone bends to her book again.

Finally she feels the motor turn over, rev and rumble. It's the intake of breath of a woman behind her that makes her look up just in time to see the door begin to close and to hear the gasp of the hydraulics. The huge man who had thrown the chair is in the driver's seat. The lumberjack plaid of his shirt strains over his hunched shoulders. One hand is on the handle that operates the door, and he is trying to wrench it closed, cursing "Shittershee," while the mechanism strains and wheezes. In the door is wedged the furious little gnome body of the driver. There is a stunned paralysis in the bus. Then the door flies open and the little driver lands like a pit bull. He grabs the huge man by his shirt and wheels him out of his chair. He slams him against the windshield and flings him backward out the door. The man lands in the tarred parking lot, the driver straddling him, flailing at his hands. The passengers are half up, straining toward that side of the bus. The black boy is in the open door, and when the huge man makes a superhuman hump of himself to throw his attacker off, the boy grips the doorframe as if to brace for a leap. But falters. He looks wildly around. Does he dare make himself a hero by attacking a white man, however crazy? Leather-vest stands up in the aisle. He lifts his palm, a gesture of authority and warning. The boy, his upper body still pitched forward in the door, grips the frame and checks himself again.

By now a pair of truckers have come to the driver's aid, and the plaid shirt is pinned to the asphalt like a struggling bug. The moment passes, as most such moments pass, and Simone knows she was not breathing because she breathes again. The black boy crumples dejected into his seat beside his radio. Leather-vest stands a moment more and then he, too, sits. A sheriff's car squeals in from the highway; two cops get out. It takes four altogether to cuff the huge man and fold him, yelling his gibberish of twisted curses, down into the back seat. The car drives off, siren wailing. The heroes smooth their shirts.

This has taken three, four minutes. The bus passengers applaud. The driver checks his watch with a modest swagger. "I reckon we can make up the time between here and Louisville." The youth slumps over his radio. *For the times they are a-changin.*

As if to deny this, Leather-vest leans across to the hatted ladies. "Uppity," he says, using a woman's word for them.

"Was he going to throw himself on that man?" asks one, incredulous.

"You change the law," says Leather-vest, "and you asking for all kind of uppity."

And the woman nods. "People never change."

Which must be so, Simone thinks; everybody says it. Yet surely people do nothing else but change. Children grow up into adulterers, scholars are corrupted by ambition, louts evolve into experts on Etruscan pottery. We are cobbled together like Polonius' drama—historical-comical-tragical-pastoral.

When dark falls they are slicing through the southern tip of Indiana, twenty-six hours toward her destination. The bus is mostly quiet now, but you can hear the petulant note of the girl in the yellow dress. The boy is placating at first but increasingly querulous; at Evansville he goes into the restaurant alone to fetch his hamburger.

At St. Louis the two of them separate. They hoist their suitcases and stagger in opposite directions. The driver yawns and gathers his gear for another change of command. The fat man takes his gun down, returns it to the belt underneath his vest, and mildly disappears into the night.

She sleeps a little. When she wakes they are crossing The Big Muddy from the edge of nowhere to the middle of nowhere. In the prairie flats she thinks for a hallucinatory moment it is snowing until she realizes this is the warm ejaculation of the cottonwood trees. The suffocating night air rings with cricket sound. At dawn they pass a wide porch in a clearing of oaks where men sit like postcard art, boots on the railing, spitting into the dirt, a yellow dog asleep on the floorboards. She has come overland to limbo of her own free will.

At Columbia, Dean Sarah Magginis of Jepson State College for the Liberal Arts wraps her in a welcoming hug. She is here to drive Simone the remaining eighty miles.

"Welcome to Mis'ry," Dean Magginis says.

ANNIE, LITTLE ITALY, NEW YORK CITY, 1979.
PHOTOGRAPH BY ELI REICHMAN.

Three Poems

A L B E R T   G O L D B A R T H

Last Song

I choose the other way,
with heels dug in.
I vote for screaming

yearningly. For heading to the afterlife
against the grain of this one. For a slowing down
to the pace of a person too absorbed
in the glory and grit
to work up any hurry for departing it.
I choose greedily looking backward
at each freestone peach and grubby radiator cap,
each watermelon seed and hypodermic needle,
jonquil, castanet, railroad spike. And even so,
by now—I'm seventy-two—I've seen enough

to know that there are ample reasons
of psychology and circumstance for a quiet,
accepting, meltaway transition
from this plane of muscle and capillary
and Shakespeare's plays and Afro-plaited hair.
I choose the other way,

remembering the adamant drag
of Rembrandt's burin over the resistant surface,
bringing out a crown of light
over Jesus's head, as well as the granary shadows
rats make more rats in.
He was true to these: precise, and with integrity.
With ardor.
I want to snag in the folds like a burr.

I want to remora
onto the bellyflesh of creation.
Every anther. Every pollen grain, that under
magnification resembles the Taj Mahal.
And the Taj Mahal. The grouting—not much different
from yours or mine—that's necessary even in
the Taj Mahal. If I must go, I want my teethmarks

on the inner velvet nap of nearby tree bark, saying
I went, but in a frenzy of refusal. Let me be a squatter
standing with a shotgun in the doorway labeled Breath.
I want to be a cult—if only a cult of only me—
that won't vacate the compound. I choose to be stubborn,
I want to be full-on jackass stubborn over Einstein's
spidery scrimmage of equations, over the gelid mass
of a fresh lung in the transplant tray, I choose to be a miser
of jewels and breasts, of sewage treatment plants.
An inch cube of beryllium. A scimitar hilt.
An alligator pear.
The *no* of Rosa Parks, on loan to me.
I want to be witnessed

floating above the hospital bed, still tethered
by the paying-out tube of a catheter

the way the astronaut's corded
to the mother ship on a space walk.
I want to be witnessed,
witnessed rising to the ceiling
still attached by that stem.
I want to be unwilling.

Persist

The way that Whitney Houston
could extend a final note, extend
the word inside that final note, like some
ethereal taffy being pulled out of her lungs
and up to the stars, or a wire extended
into invisibility and yet
its tensile strength would slice your heart in two . . .
that's how it is: we won't let go,
our overwhelming and formative passions
ask that we hold on to them still,
and still more, and still aftermath more,
they ache for the dig of our fingernails,
they want our tongue to fasten like a remora.
A bouquet still floats above
the long-gone shelf life date, and the contrail feathers
still embellish the sky when the jet has disappeared.
And Ishmael . . . ?
When the operatically epic voyage
ends, and the *Pequod* sinks, and all of its voices
drown, a final note still lingers,
clings like a barnacle to its rolling spar
—a persistence that carries a novel inside.

———————

Three Unalike-Like Scenarios

That lame-ass shit-on-his-dick motherfucker
goddam cheated on her *again*
with Miss Skank Waitress 2019? She will *KILL* him.
And across town, Mr. Trusting Soul just realizes
Bimbo Bitch has slipped his credit card out
of his wallet a jillionth time. . . . The thing is, though,
the scorch-your-soul thing is, that neither
of these beleaguered two can ever give up
their addictive love; and the chimera hope
of reforming the Other persists,
persists, persists, persists. . . . /

                              In I.C.U. our friend R.
won't give up. The ward is a twenty-room-long
hush, punctuated by pompom bursts
of agonized moaning. R. won't sign
the Do Not Resuscitate form. R. won't relinquish
her love for every stained glass masterpiece
with the sun in Jesus's crown of thorns, and
picnic ant, and clawhead hammer, and book club nosh,
and mandolin string, and rivet, and divot
the planet has to offer. The tiny maze in a fresh-burst
kernel of popcorn suddenly looks as gorgeous to her
as an orchid's extravagant spirals.
She won't yield an inch;
she won't unplug the song of who she is,
or turn off the *reverb* button.
She so fiercely lusts to retain
her physical place in this physical world,
it feels counterintuitive to call it
"preparing to be a ghost."

And yet isn't that exactly what a ghost *is?*
Something that can't let go. /

And from MIT:
"Researchers have developed a system for converting all molecular
structures of proteins into audible sound that resembles musical
passages. Any protein's long sequence of amino acids becomes a
sequence of notes. Then, reversing the process, they can introduce
some variations into the music *and convert it back into proteins
never before seen in nature* [my emphasis]."

  To trail a glissando across a keyboard of proteins!
  Composer, year 2050: protein arpeggios!

"Different aspects of [the information by which proteins function]
can now be encoded in a form that humans are particularly well-attuned
to, [the music of] pitch, volume, and duration."

  Ah. Duration.
  I'm seventy-two, and if any of this
  incredible bio-magic might
  increase our human longevity…
  hurry up, MIT, put a little
  pep in your daily lab routine!

———————

When R., a former
high school music teacher, finally died,
she was holding some sheet music
tightly against her chest,
and her fingers on the ruled staves
made it look as if she were playing guitar

for her last act here on the Earth.
Air guitar, I guess. And then,
in a while, she was air herself.
                                    In the grave
of Queen Shub-ad at Ur, that eminence
was found on her bier with the bodies
of two women attendants positioned
"one at the head and one at the foot."
Human sacrifices. Also there,
a man's skeleton—the court harpist.
"His arm bones were still lying across
his broken instrument, with its bull's head
of gold and lapis lazuli, which
he evidently had been holding fast
even as he died."
We can't know what his music meant to him.
But we do know he wouldn't let go.

Astronomy Song, with Confusions

An earlier version of this obituary misstated the name of Mr.
Hoagland's first poetry collection. It is "Sweet Ruin," not
"Sweet Rain."
                                        —*The New York Times*

They look, they *are*, so unapproachable
and indifferent; still, it's because of the stars
that sometimes we don't even know if we're suffering

or easing over the borderline into a day
of lazy contentment. We're created
from their energy and matter, as you know, and so
what we would see as major realignments
of those ur-components (Democrat/Republican
for example, Bird of Paradise/piranha
for example) they would understand
as equivalent Big Bang units
indistinguishably shaped. And you can tell me
that the woman who's wrestled her camel,

finally, strenuously, onto the sand and sheltered
against the coming simoom in the part-enclosing nook
of its belly, the camelstink rising as heavy now
as prongs inside her nostrils . . . and the woman being paid
a thousand dollars tonight for Super Rap Dude X
to snort a line of champagne-quality cocaine
from the velvety valley between her breasts

. . . are many galaxies apart in degree,
in basic Homo sapiens degree, but go ahead, tell that
to the stars comprising Andromeda, see if their spectra
blink by a single potassium molecule,
shout it, go ahead. The ink
of King's "I have a dream" oration / the ink

of *Mein Kampf*. Use astral
measurements, and sex and death are closer

than the breathing pores along the sides of a cockroach
and the "great red spot" on Jupiter, which are brother and sister
atoms, after all. By astral metrics,
sex and death are twined irrevocably and the same

electrochemical substrata hold
them both. And yet we know, we *know*,
the difference. Our lowest depravity
(remember that night? remember that thought
that night?) and our saintliest innocence . . .
we *know*—duh—how to tell one from the other; but don't
expect Betelguese to care. The genome,

the same one genome, was lizard
then bird then gill-thing in the womb and now
is you; and *I'm* amazed, but don't look to Cassiopeia
to grovel at that or do jumping jacks.
Public *and* private?—every one of us,
whether painfully or with suavity, bilocates
here-there-here a hundred times across a day, although
we're homogenous substance to the Milky Way.
Oh really? You can have this arm

I'm writing with, stars, if you'll keep my wife
—my singular, unduplicatable wife—
from harm. My wife in the light,
my wife in the indigo thunderstorm.

It's a monstrous thought, I know:
to the laws of thermodynamics, evil and good
are identical twins.

Depending on the metric, error

might not exist: mistakes imply comparatives at work,
but the stars are inclined to see
all forms as Form; if we want to be people
and not some pure embodiment of "astral stuff,"
we might have to cherish mistakeness.
It could be that we're never dead any more

than we're alive; it's all just cyclic recombinings
of an Oort cloud's (Google it) elements
with some one-way-or-another physics
giving a directional tilt to the mix. That may
be true, but it has little to do

with mourning or with pleasure—really *anything*
we call "human" and feel owns us
overwhelmingly in the groin, or the meaty cathedral
we label "the heart," or our pinprick tear ducts.
Today I was thinking of Tony Hoagland

and the rain came down,
no the sun, no the rain, oh the sweet,
the ruinous, the sweet, sweet rain.

Contagion

W I L L I A M   T R O W B R I D G E

*Let's hope we don't catch it. I'd hate to wake up some
morning and find out that you weren't you.*
> —Invasion of the Body Snatchers

Some squares are really circles, Daddy said.
They're round inside but hide it cleverly—
a snaky trait, and maybe it could spread.

They have no point so might as well be dead.
Alive they put us all in jeopardy:
those squares are circled round us, Daddy said.

It clearly has to do with how they're bred,
not like us, who do with qualms and brevity
that seamy act whose germs they're known to spread.

What makes them act that way we dread
to talk about, it shakes our poise so readily.
Some squares would make us circles, Daddy said.

We'd like to take them to the backyard shed
and whip them till their backside's leathery.
And hesitating only helps it spread.

The slippery slope they hope to have us sled
we fear as much as death or even bankruptcy.
Some squares are really circles, Daddy said,
and feeling round some nights, we fear it's spread.

HAIRPINS, BREATHITT COUNTY, KENTUCKY.
PHOTOGRAPH BY GLORIA BAKER FEINSTEIN.

Captain Elvis

MICHAEL HENSON

S he was a young girl with enormous eyes, and she was bumming change on the sidewalk by the drugstore in the mall. Resting, she became very small and her eyes looked sharp as those of a fox. Whenever a man approached, or even a boy who looked like he might give up a quarter, her eyes widened to the far ends of her face. She said, in a husky mumble, "Excuse me, do you have any change?" or, if he were younger, "Hey, man, you got some change?" She cupped her hand, very small.

She was a pale young woman, made even paler by her black leather jacket. And paler yet by her dark, precise, almost blackish lipstick and the slash of rouge across each cheek. Her lashes were dark; she had carefully penciled black liner around each eye. She wore blue jeans slashed at each knee. When she stretched out her hand, the sleeve of her jacket pulled back to show a ring of blue thorns tattooed onto her wrist.

Each of the men who stopped dug into his pocket for a moment, pulled up a small stack of quarters, dimes, or nickels, held them in the tips of his fingers, then dropped them into the cup of her palm. Then quickly, as if this encounter had made him late, he hustled into the parking lot, or into the drugstore, or around the corner to the video store, or down the mall corridor toward the grocery, the shoe store, the fitness center, or the Chinese carryout.

"Thank you," she murmured. Or, "Thanks, man." She jingled the change a moment in the cup of her palm before she dropped the coins into the pocket of her jacket.

She tried women as well, but less enthusiastically and with no success. The women moved behind a wall of glass. Each stared at the girl with something like pity; but none of them turned over any money.

The mall sat at the edge of a college campus and at the edge of a neighborhood divided into black and white areas. Beyond the mall, there was a street lined with bars, shops, restaurants, and clubs. It was all busy and people had change to spare if they would. At the center of the mall, an open-air court fronted various shops. A covered walkway formed a corridor from the parking lot of the drugstore, past the courtyard, to the parking lot of the grocery. The young woman stood at the drugstore end of the corridor and leaned against a pillar.

It was a Friday night. A cold Friday night for April. Odd tricks of wind skipped the cold down the corridor and around the corners of the mall and caused her to draw up like an animal into its den. Her shoulders narrowed and she tucked her chin into the collar of her jacket.

It should have been a good night to be hustling for change. The college crowd was out for the nightclubs. The black kids from the neighborhood were out for the streets. Working people who had just gotten paid tugged their children behind them to the grocery. Vans, little foreign cars, shining SUVs, and old, low-slung, rumbling hoopties cruised through the parking lot, searching for a place to park, pumping out rap, rock 'n' roll, and country in a great stir of radio noise.

She was not the only one looking for change. Just outside the mall, a slender man carried a baby bottle and approached people to tell how his car had broken down and he and his wife and baby were stuck here a hundred miles from home and could you . . . And a man in a black suit and a clerical collar approached to tell about the good work of his church and could you . . . And a woman would follow a person down the street—very excited, for she had been clean off of crack cocaine for ninety days and the welfare was going to give her children back and some nice person just gave her ten dollars and could you . . .

A security guard worked the mall each night. Some nights, there was a nice one, but not this night, not this guard. This one dogged her; she had seen him before. So, without seeming to watch, she watched for him. Each time he rounded a corner into sight, she boosted herself up from the pillar and moved away. The real police were all right; every half hour or so, a big white cruiser floated through the parking lot. One or the other of the officers inside stared at her a moment as if she were a picture on a wall. They knew what she was doing, but they never bothered her.

This security guard meant business. He was a thin, little, puffed-up man who wore a white shirt, shiny with starch. Big black patches on his shoulders were stitched with golden eagles and the name of his company. She had never let him catch up with her, but she knew that if he caught her bumming change among the mall customers, he would have her busted. At the very least, he would bump her from the mall property. He would break her if he could. She could tell; she knew that kind of person. So she always avoided him. She always stayed one step ahead. The guard would be harder to spot tonight. Because of the chill, he wore a black nylon jacket over the starched, white shirt with the black patches and the gold letters. If she did not watch, he would steal up on her like a Ninja.

She glanced again and saw no sign of him. A man was leaving the drugstore with a plastic bag in each hand.

"Excuse me. Do? . . ."

He shook his head quickly, picking up his pace. They hardly ever stopped if both hands were full.

A black woman pushed past with all her children behind her in a row, each one lugging a grocery bag. The girl met eyes with the woman a moment, felt a strong challenging current, and did not even think of asking her for change. The woman walked by and shook her head and muttered back to the children who each raised and dropped his or her eyes as they passed.

A family of Pakistanis, a half-dozen skinheads, some old people pulling wire grocery carts behind them: nothing. The wind cut through the tunnel, and she jammed her hands into her pockets and ducked into the collar of her jacket.

A man in glasses and a baseball jacket came out whistling. When she leaned forward to him and asked, he handed her twenty-three cents. She slipped the money into her pocket and jingled what was there. She hesitated to count her money; it seemed like bad luck. But she knew she was short.

This sucks, she thought. She began to pace back and forth in front of her pillar. Three rounds, and she stopped a biker who gave her fifty cents.

The next guy wore a hooded sweatshirt and was stocky as a brick. He grinned, soon as he saw her, as if he had been waiting just for her. Instead of his pocket, he reached for his crotch. He leaned at her as he passed. "I got something for you," he said.

"Stick it in your fist," she muttered. She spat, then made ready for the next.

Once, finally, a woman, a weasely old woman with hair as silky as a mink, actually did give her money—a quarter, a nickel, and a column of pennies.

"Thank you," the girl mumbled. She turned and made ready to lean toward a frat-house-looking guy with a six-pack under his arm.

But the old woman gripped her at the elbow. "Honey, I used to be in the same, exact situation as you. I did. Then I got right with Jesus."

The girl smiled at the old woman and nodded, then turned to look away. She had been taught to respect old people, even if they pulled you by the coat, even if they smelled like dead trees, even if they talked all crazy, and even if they cost you an unknown quantity of quarters still warming in the pocket of the fraternity dude.

"Jesus will take care of you, honey. You just have to ask. He's all around us. He's everywhere." She smiled. But she kept her little fist pincered into the girl's elbow.

"Okay, Ma'am. Thank you." The girl pulled gently against the old woman's pincers. A man had to step around them. She leaned toward him and said, "Pardon me. . . . " But the old woman still gripped her at the elbow and the man got past.

"When I was young . . ." the old woman continued. The girl had spotted a guy with long, gray hair tied back, leaving the Chinese carryout with a bag in one hand. She knew he was a good mark and, with a glance to check for the shadowy little guard, made her face ready.

But the old woman still hung onto her elbow. "I tell you," she said. "I did all sorts of wild things."

The girl nodded and continued to pull against the woman's grip. The ponytail man went by without looking her way, trailing an odor of soy sauce and hot cardboard.

The old woman pulled down hard on the girl's elbow and buzzed into the girl's ear. "I hitch-hiked. I rode rail cars. I did a lot of things a girl wasn't supposed to do."

Two more men passed out of the drugstore, but the girl was still snagged on the old woman's fist. It was just as well, for she spotted, at the other end of the tunnel, a slim pencil of darkness rounding the corner of the grocery. She knew by the cap and the little glint of gold at the shoulders that it was the guard.

"Wherever I went, Jesus was always with me," the old woman said. She gave the girl's elbow a sharp squeeze.

"That's deep," the girl said. The guard was advancing, checking in the window of each shop and eye-balling each hip-hop kid who passed.

"Excuse me," she said. She made her voice gentle but firm. "I've got to go now." She placed her hand on the hand of the older woman and noted how cold the hand was, how small and hard and cold.

The guard had come halfway down the corridor; he was passing the door of the health-food store.

"Bye now," said the old woman.

"Yeah," said the girl. She walked toward the video store, as if she meant to get a movie, then turned and cut around to the back lot of the grocery.

A tractor-trailer had backed into the loading bay, and she could hear the crates and boxes rattling down the conveyors and the shouts of the crew loading them onto skids. She would not look, but she knew that the men of the crew jabbed each other with their elbows, pointed at her, and laughed.

She turned the corner, crossed the parking lot, passed the door of the grocery and entered the little plaza across from the mall. The plaza had a set of concrete benches, potted trees, and a dry fountain. A grocery cart had been drawn loose of the grocery lot. Crippled by the loss of a wheel, it lay on its side, its ribs gleaming in the lamplight. A half-dozen skateboarders in their big shirts and ball caps had gathered to watch each other vault the carcass of the grocery cart and to grind the corners of the fountain.

"Wassup," one called to her. He was a heavy boy, with big round shoulders and a soft, moonish face. He dropped his board, positioned his left foot on the deck, kicked off, pushed six times for power, then lifted off, graceful in spite of his size and sailed over the cart.

He landed with knees bent and arms spread and his face stony and serene.

"Wassup," he called again. He caught up with her halfway across the plaza. "Remember me?"

She shrugged. The skater followed her to the edge of the plaza, and they stood waiting for a walk light.

"Why don't you hang with us for a while?"

"I got to get some money."

"Aw, come on, man."

She looked at him, cold and cutting.

"Whatever," he shrugged.

She had tired of waiting for the light and stepped out into the street ahead of him.

He dropped his board, skated past her, then stopped at the curb. "Come hang out with us later on," he said. "We'll go get a pizza."

She nodded, and he skated back across the street.

Her plan was to head up Vine. She took up a spot down the street from the theater to catch the movie crowd. It was between shows; traffic there was slow. So she moved across the street to the bar where a band was warming up, but the baby-bottle man had already worked that crowd. She found a good position outside the coffee shop, but the saved-from-crack lady sailed into the first couple out the door with her ten-dollar bill flying, and announced, "You know I been released from the program and I got my own apartment, and I ain't doing that crack no more. And people been so nice to me! I used to think all white people was prejudiced, but look, this lady give me this ten dollar bill to go and get me some groceries. She was, like, get you some decent food and build yourself back up, and now I'm getting my weight back, thank the Lord. And if I had five more dollars, I could get . . . Why thank you! You know if I had just that one extra dollar I . . . Why thank you! Thank you! You are sooo sweet!"

So she crossed the street and reentered the mall. She scouted the area for a sign of the little gold-shouldered guard, then retook her station at the pillar. Twenty minutes later, she was cold and luckless and had grown steadily more tired. Steps and voices continued to echo in the corridor and the wind continued to crowd her. But she could not yet quit.

A man appeared at the center of the tunnel. He walked with brisk, square steps and he covered his ground quickly. He was a block-shouldered, thin-haired, wide-eyed, jowly man in a suit and an open overcoat. He must not have noticed her, for when she pulled herself up from the pillar, set her eyes wide, and leaned toward him, he stopped—startled—as if she had leveled a gun on him. His eyes—pale blue eyes guarded by thin gray brows—narrowed. He made a half-step backward.

"Excuse me . . ." She cupped her hand. "Can you spare some change?" She made sure her voice had that husky note.

He immediately relaxed. His eyes widened. "Well," he said. "Quite a wind tonight, isn't it?"

She nodded and waited as he pushed back his overcoat, and began to dig in his pocket. She saw a square blue name tag pinned to his lapel and realized he was the manager of the drugstore, changing shift, heading home.

He was smiling, his eyes fixed on a point just past her cupped palm. He held up a half dollar between forefinger and thumb, but he did not turn it loose.

She glanced right and left for the guard. The manager might be trying to hold her attention until the guard came around.

"If I give you this money," he asked, "what do you plan to do with it?"

She glanced right and left. "I need to get a cab to get home."

"And where's home?"

She shrugged. She tried to think of a name.

"You're not going to use this for drugs, are you?"

She made a distasteful look and shook her head.

He pressed the coin into her palm and nodded toward her wrist, "What does the tattoo mean?"

"The tattoo?" She looked down at her chain of thorns. "It doesn't mean anything. It's just a tattoo."

"Why thorns? Why not something? . . ."

"I don't know." She looked past him down the corridor. "It's just a tattoo."

"But it's odd. Thorns. At first I thought it was a bracelet."

She shrugged.

He leaned closer and whispered.

"What?" He had whispered so quickly that she did not understand.

He leaned closer and spoke slowly, deliberately, and with a sidelong surreptitious glance. "Do you," he asked, "have any other? . . ."

"Do I what?"

He leaned forward again. "Do you have tattoos in any other places?"

She sharpened her eyes and dropped her helpless look. She dodged to get around him. "I sure wouldn't show them to you." She walked several steps before the coin in her hand began to feel foul. She turned, walked back, and stretched the coin out to him. "Take your little money. I don't need it."

But he retracted his hand, as if she had reached out to swipe him with a kitchen rag. He turned on his heel, and hurried off into the parking lot.

She wanted to drill the coin into his back, but in a moment, he was lost among the cars in the parking lot. She looked at the coin in her open palm. It's money, she thought. I earned it. She started to drop it into her pocket, but the coin felt foul. So she cocked her arm like a pitcher and flung it high into the air. It caught a single spangle of lamplight it as it fell and hit the roof of a car.

*   *   *

The pair of police officers, the real police, floated around the parking lot in their cruiser, gazing over the Chinese couple with their happy baby, the black boys in their high tops and gold, the red-faced man in his ragged jeans jacket, and the college students with their ball caps pulled down close to their eyes. The officers studied closely the bearded man in biker's leather, the black children who ran from customer to customer asking could they carry their packages, and the pale girl who leaned against the pillar near the door of the drugstore. Of all the people coming and going in the mall, they studied her most closely.

To someone who did not know, they looked as if they were gazing through her, as if she were water. In fact, they saw everything about her. The girl, from the corner of her eye, saw them cruise past and saw that they watched her.

They're okay, she thought. It was that little rent-a-cop that was the problem. The real police had never bothered her.

She did not see the officers stop the cruiser and get out. She did not see them approach her at her station, one from each side of the pillar so, just as she was setting herself to lean toward a big, trucker-looking man with his arms full of groceries, she was faced with the police in stereo—one officer on each side.

They closed themselves toward her like a set of double doors.

"Just hold it right there, miss," said the near one. The other looked around to the mall.

"What'd I do?"

"Do you have some I.D.?" The one who spoke had a thick, brushy mustache.

"It's at home," she said.

"Where's home?"

She shrugged. "I can go get it," she offered.

The radio on the shoulder of the clean-shaven officer squawked like a parrot, and he lifted his hand toward it. "Copy," he answered.

The radio spoke again in radio-pidgin.

"We have a complaint of solicitation at the mall," he answered. "Suspect is white, female, age between sixteen and twenty. We're interviewing her now. Over."

"What?" she demanded. "What do you mean, solicitation?"

The officer looked away and continued to talk into the radio. "What does he mean?" she said to the other.

"We've had a complaint," said the officer through his mustache, "about a white female fitting your description soliciting customers outside the drugstore."

"I've been bumming change. That's it."

"And you can't produce any I.D?"

"I told you. It's at the house where I'm staying."

"Where are you staying?"

"I'm crashing with some friends. Look, I'll go get it right now."

"But where do you live?"

"I'm here visiting . . ."

"And so, you live . . ."

"I'm from out of town . . ."

"So you're here to take in the wonderful atmosphere." His eyes panned across the whole of the mall, with its cars, noise, lights, and hustling people. His face was a perfect mask of contempt.

"Can I go now?"

"Not just yet."

"I haven't done anything wrong."

"That's not what we heard."

"What did you hear?"

"We've had a complaint from the manager of this store that you've been trying to hustle his customers."

"That's a lie."

"We have a complaint that you have tried to solicit sex for pay from this spot and that customers have complained to security."

She began to choke with fear. "That's a lie," she said again. "He's the motherfucker that tried to hustle me."

At a nod from the mustached cop, the clean-shaven cop put his hand to his radio again. "We have a young female,

white, apparently under eighteen. No identification. No
known local address. Possible runaway. Over."

The radio squawked back.

"Pretty uncooperative. We're gonna bring her in for
some questions. Over."

The girl shrank back against her pillar and made herself
very small. She seemed to press herself down into the
bricks. Her head sank down into her shoulders and her
eyes narrowed and darted back and forth. She became even
paler than before; she turned pale as salt.

"She's not a hooker. I've been watching her," said a thin,
clipped voice. The little security guard stood rocking on his
heels. The near officer looked at him briefly, then continued
to enter notes into his pad.

"I see her all the time," the guard said. He stood with
his thumbs hooked into his belt, cowboy style, very straight.
Neither of the real police would look at him.

"She's out here every night, bumming change, but she
never bothers anybody."

"That's not what your boss thinks." The near officer
spoke without looking up from his notebook.

"What boss?"

"The manager here." The officer nodded toward the
drugstore.

"He's not my boss." He gave them the name of his
security company. "I'm telling you, I watch her. I watch all
these kids. I know which ones are trouble and which ones
are okay. This one, I just try to keep her moving."

The officers looked at one another, but neither looked at
the security guard. The shorter one heard a new message
on his shoulder radio; he turned aside to listen and respond.
The near one finished his note and clapped his notepad
shut. He waited, as the shorter officer continued to listen to
his new message. With a nod, the shorter officer indicated
the street outside the mall, and the near one said to the girl,
"Okay, you can go."

The girl looked from one officer to the other. Could she trust what she had just heard? She looked to the security guard with the gold patches on his shoulders, then back to the officers who were no longer concerned with her. In a moment, she had disappeared like smoke.

*   *   *

Under the lights of Vine Street, a young woman leaned against a wooden fence painted gray and marked again and again with graffiti. She was a small young woman, made even smaller by the way she shrank into her jacket for warmth, and pale, made even paler by the milky lights that fell from the lamps up and down the street.

With her was a heavy boy in loose, baggy clothes standing with a skateboard tucked under his arm. He was taller than the girl, but no older. Moving only his eyes, he watched the traffic on the street as if he were on duty.

At a glance, they seemed to be just another set of figures and frames painted on the wall.

In a bar nearby, a band was playing; the building itself seemed to throb. Whenever the doors opened, the girl watched to see which way those coming out would turn.

The door opened, the guitar sang out, the drum kit rattled, and the singer's voice swelled. A couple came out, and the girl turned to look. The couple turned left, walking briskly to beat the cold to their car. The girl boosted herself up from the wall, cupped her palm, and asked, "Can you spare? . . ."

The man shook his head no. He wore a short leather jacket and gloves; his hair was cropped close and square. The woman had sculpted her hair so that it puffed up and fell down just so; her make-up was just so; her heels and her tight skirt and her jacket were just so. She had her arm hooked into the arm of her date, but she looked back at the girl with a look something like pity.

The girl leaned back against the wall and pulled herself into her jacket. She did not look back at the couple again.

"It's this cold weather, man," he said. "People don't want to stop and give it up when it's cold like this."

She wiped at her nose with a little bit of napkin.

"Man, if it was warm, they'd be going, like pop, pop, pop. They'd be showing you some money. Now it's, like, I just want to get in my little yuppie car and go."

The couple had, in fact, gotten into a red, four-wheel drive wagon. The skater watched, but the girl did not.

"What time is it?" the girl asked.

"I don't know, man. It's late."

Several cars passed, low-riders, pickup trucks, every kind of car, even a white stretch limousine with darkened windows. But no one walked the sidewalk.

"So, he just told you to move on, didn't he?"

"Who?"

"Captain Elvis."

"Who?"

"That security guard dude."

She said nothing. She pulled her jacket closer.

"Captain Elvis. The little king."

"Is that his name?"

"He doesn't have a name. He's just Captain E."

She rubbed her arms for the cold and said nothing.

"He's all right. He just does that to keep the stores from freaking out. He doesn't mess with us much."

She looked away. She even boosted herself up to look past him.

"Man, you ought to give it up out here," the boy said.

She remained silent and watched all corners of the street.

"You got a place you can go? Why don't you get warmed up?"

She rubbed her arms again for the cold and said nothing.

"Man, you ought to give it up."

She looked past him, up the street and down.

"If you don't have a place you can go, me and my friends, we can hook you up."

She turned and leaned on one shoulder so as to show him her back. She watched nothing but the street. Music continued coming from the nightclubs up and down the street and from the speakers of cars. Up and down the block there was traffic and talk and laughter. Yet all she had was a little pocketful of change. Not enough for a meal, not enough for a little taste of weed. The wind kicked up. The cold pierced her like a talon. She shivered against the gray wall. Pale, darkly marked, needled by penitential thorns, she stood at her station as if watched by an invisible guard.

HINTERLANDS, 2015.
PHOTOGRAPH BY ELI REICHMAN.

Two Poems

G E O R G E   K A L A M A R A S

The Mother Door of Forgiveness

Based on two photographs of Ben Lilly—the last of the true mountain men—and his hounds, circa 1917 and 1920.

"A hound's face always looks mournful . . ."

—Jim Kjelgaard, *Lion Hound*

Sad, is all I can say. The hounds look sad. Jack, Crook,
Tip, and Queen. They hunted the mountain lion
for their man. And all their joy, afterward, flooded out,
into him, lengthening his beard an inch or two more
down his mountain-man chest. What are they thinking,
staring up at the carcass of what was once an angry god?
How do they feel now that the power's gone out, the lion stretched
on a pole before them, claw to claw, tongue to tail, as if trapped—
mid-stride—streaming out into the universe? The roar,
quiet as a single cactus beckoning the rain for a desert
bloom. If the dogs could, they'd ask for fig leaves. Storm forth
from the garden of houndly delight. Bowed and begging. Shame.
Shame on Ben Lilly, standing there proud.
This is El Paso or Chihuahua. Or maybe an unnamed ranch
west of Chloride, New Mexico. Some speck
as indistinct on a map as an unwept tear in a cup.
I want to cut it down, bury the cat by *not* burying it,
placing it in a night tree—a branch of burr oak—offering its bones
as a flute to the wind-dead. As milk back to the chalky moon.
Its hide as medicine wrap. *Big* medicine. I want to hug the hounds
tightly, saying, *I, too, have regret. Only so much of me
has done the world any good. Of my sixty-three years,
I'd say it was a month or two at most. And of those days,
I gave mostly just a kind word. Often unheard.*
You were asked to kill, and you killed too well. Your long ears
swaying as if the wind were the released breath of a world

sighing goodnight. Goodnight Ben, and your .30-30 Winchester
and Green River skinning knife. Goodnight lion ears,
having to endure all that howling for days and days
on your track. Goodnight cliff ledge, where—finally—
the cornered cat's last step was final as the thud
that broke its back. Goodnight Jack. Goodnight Crook.
Goodnight Tip and Queen. You were thrown
by a long line of amorous sires not knowing one day
you'd be thrust into your own sad hearts.
You came through the mother door
of female forgiveness that suckled you and ate your pup poop
and licked all the starlight of womb water off of you
when you dropped from eternity among us
into the four corners of the whelping box. The corners of one
world hunting another. Keeping you with us. Here.
Close to our grief. And regret. Where each day of the hunt
your joy bursts forth. Fractures. Your sadness
blooms. As you mourn the dead thing
in front of you. Again and again.

There Are Many Moods Swimming
Through the Dark

So I bonded with the hound—the way old
hunters had advised—spit into its mouth
when a pup and let my essence drip down
its gullet, almost like a stone sinking
into the still, slow mud of the Wabash.
The old-timers seemed to chew barbed wire.
The sound of rust in their bones voiced dredged years,
midnights of full moons and empty arms. Yes,
part of me keeps falling into what I
most love. Into the ruinous, white waves
of the Wabash promising to cleanse my
bones with light from campfires slowed with cold.
What I hope to one day postulate is
a posture of knowing when *not* to know,

if love be a way of loving love's loss.
Please, you say, *I hear Wang Wei in your veins*.
Discipline of river reeds. Disciple
of breath. Mentor of milk in sad mountain
moons. There are many moods in this old heart.
And one of those moods—though we've not yet met—
is you. Your red hair. Your long lovely legs.
I find in you the essence of redbone
coonhounds who sniff the woods as they become
the world. To spit in the eye of every
cliché. To rise, sloe-eyed, at the crack of
nines. Dressed to the dawns. We say it so much
and cruel, our words reverse. Light swimming through
the dark's dark in a hound dog's midnight snout.

Two Poems

KAREN KOVACIK

Self-Portrait with Litany of Saints

As a child, I folded my arms in an X
to be like Gabriel,

wings crossed in front,
my fluffy purple rug a cloud.

I could memorize anything: catechism
of destiny and free will, prayers

dangerous as spells. "Hallowèd."
"Most grievous fault." "Commit me here."

Sometimes I'd pose like statues
of saints. Bridget who willed herself

ugly. Peter crucified upside down.
Sebastian with arrows galore.

Catherine who feasted on nothing
but the Lord.

* * *

At fifteen when I learned to fast
and my periods stopped

my mother took me to her doctor.
There I studied colorful posters

on the trimesters of pregnancy.
"Blessed is the fruit of her womb."

I took off my pants under a harsh halo,
slid my heels in the stirrups

and suffered the cold steel
unto me. Saint Lucy cradling

her jellied eyes on a plate.
Saint Agatha shorn of her breasts.

* * *

Then for years I lived like a Magdalene,
my bed a chapel of sandalwood and wine,

where I wrestled with angels, fat nipples
of fuchsia sunning themselves on the terrace.

My palms would ache like stigmata
when we loved each other all afternoon.

Saint Afra, who ran a bordello.
Saint Christina the Astonishing

who dissolved into air. Saint Augustine
who asked the cup of chastity to pass him by.

* * *

Work became my cell,
my beloved desert. I tilled

in silence and harvested,
singing. Swept up fronds

of words, shaped psalms
from stunted wheat.

Saint John the Dwarf, who watered
parched wood till it flowered

into fruit. Saint Macarius,
who lit the dark with his face.

I went untouched for years
and did not die.

* * *

Now in this grotto of massage
I lay myself down on a soft altar.

The woman who works on me
is Clare, named for the saint

who sawed off her braid
and relinquished her silks for a coarse robe.

This Clare cracks my trapezius
and cloaks my spine in oil.

Saint Lawrence, blistered on the grill,
Saint Lazarus, emerging from the tomb.

Cedar on my skin, I rise from the table,
up the long stairs, and into the streets' dark nave.

Vessel, Vassal

An analysis of dental plaque illuminates
the forgotten history of female scribes.
—The Atlantic

Fire took the scrolls and codices, the illuminated Hours,
all inkpots and penknives, slanted desks and sconces,

even the oyster shells and wooden bowls for mixing paint.
Yet your secret's in your teeth, bits of blue pigment

on your incisors, color of Mary's cloak in the manger,
crushed lapis from Afghan heights via the Silk Road—

testament to your skill with fine brushes from squirrel
you'd lick to a point for a clean edge. From matins

to compline, you hardly saw the sky. Yet daily the angel
came to your desk, daily the evangelists—

John's eagle, Mark's lion, the winged man of Matthew, Luke's ox.
Did they comfort you in the season without sun,

your fingers gloved from cold? The demon acedia
spread like pestilence from this labor

to lift the sinful body in prayer,
strangely alchemized from the body's scruff:

earwax to stabilize eggwash, lead mixed with dung
steeped in vinegar to invent the purest white.

You the vessel, the handmaiden, the vassal the abbess
displayed to the wealthiest lords till your eyes dimmed

and spine slanted like script, pocks of blue on your teeth
from Noah's flood, the River Jordan, Jesus walking on the sea.

Too Bad

C A R L   D E N N I S

Too bad you met me when I was small-hearted and spiteful
And not as I am now, known for my generosity,
Someone who'd never utter the hurtful phrases
Uttered in an earlier era by a man I admit identical
To me in name and in DNA, but in nothing else.
Yes, the path from his consciousness
To my own is continuous, but marked by so many changes
In landscape and climate as it winds from a valley floor
Thorough lowland meadows to mountain freshets
It ought to be thought of as many paths, not one.
Not to answer my letters now seems like blaming a grandson
Bent on reform for the crimes of his granddad.
Shall the sins of the fathers be visited on the children
As the old law has it, or will you turn to the new law
That asks the past to bury itself while the present
Sets sail at sunrise, off to a new-found land,
A still unstoried America? What I said to you
Is as far away from my life now as the lame excuses
Offered the Cherokee and Choctaw
When America broke its word and made them nomads
Long before my grandparents landed
Looking for safer streets to open their bakery
And raise their children. Are you going to claim
That all the apologies I've written since then
Have been penned by the same man you remember?
How else am I to interpret your silence?
You'd have written back at least once to say my letters
Annoyed you if you merely wanted to be let alone.
Silence with you, I'm sorry to say, seems a strategy,
A Siren call to lure my ship into the past
And leave me lost among reefs and ice floes.
How often must I explain that it isn't working,
How often write you in a voice civil and patient,
Which only you won't accept as mine?

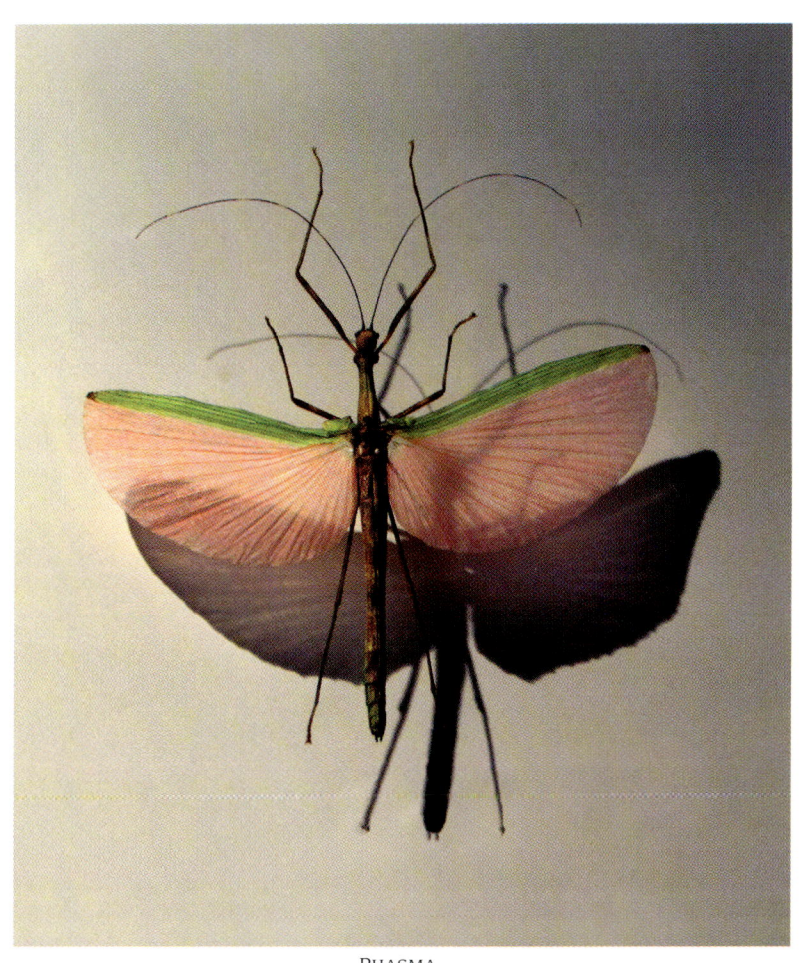

PHASMA.
PHOTOGRAPH BY CYNTHIA BEARD.

SPRING CREEK, OIL ON CANVAS,
BY CAROL ZASTOUPIL.

FLOATING WORLDS II.
PHOTOGRAPH BY REBECCA OFIESH.

BROADWAY BRIDGE, KANSAS CITY, MISSOURI, 1984.
PHOTOGRAPH BY ELI REICHMAN.

HIGH GROVE WAY, OIL ON CANVAS,
BY CAROL ZASTOUPIL.

BLUE.
PHOTOGRAPH BY REBECCA OFIESH.

Fountain Boys, 1980.
Photograph by Eli Reichman.

SUMMIT RIDGE ROAD, OIL ON CANVAS,
BY CAROL ZASTOUPIL.

Imuta

MARIE ÉTIENNE

Translated from the French by Marilyn Hacker.

Elaborated from excerpts of the interrogation of Captain Yashiboshi, known as Imuta, who was the commander of the fourth company of infantry regiment 225 stationed at Lang Son, during the trial of Japanese officers for war crimes—the execution of French prisoners of war—at the end of World War II. The documents were found by the author in the papers of her father, himself a prisoner of war, who survived.

Dated the twelfth of November at 9:45 a.m. and the fourteenth of November at 11 a.m., in the year 1946

       I was certain
that a day like today would come
       but as commanding officer
I must protect my men
       as an officer
I must protect my officers and non-commissioned officers as well

       For the execution
I can not write without being properly dressed
Give me clean clothes and two full days

       As far as Colonel Robert is concerned
from the 9th in the evening when he was taken prisoner
to the 13th, the day of his execution
       I would like to explain
       for it is my duty

* * *

I have said nothing about my soldiers
  because up until now
  I have led them
  to where there was death
(Some have fallen ill):
  I would like to return them
  to their parents
  in good health
and for them to work in a New Japan
  I beg you
  not to hold them
  responsible

Your Honor the Inspector, Your Honor the Interpreter
  forgive me

* * *

On the 9th in the evening
after I had finished my rounds
I noticed two vehicles
of the military police
they were bringing
Colonel Robert
to the campaign depot

And at approximately 8 p.m.
Colonel Robert
the Regimental Commander
and Colonel Shigume
had a discussion

*   *   *

The Regimental Commander
> Do you agree
> to surrender
> so as to avoid
> a bloodbath?

Colonel Robert
> Now that I am
> a prisoner
> I no longer have the right
> to give orders

(he rose)

Colonel Shigume
> What would you have done
> had you been
> in my place?

(I heard this conversation)

* * *

That night
the Colonel asked for a cup of tea
and went to bed
I was told that he always went calmly to sleep
on the eve of a battle
I understood that he was a great man

On the next day, the 10th,
enemy planes flew over our camp
because of them
we transferred the Colonel to the hotel in the country
where we were already holding
a couple and their children
brought there by the police

* * *

I went to see the Colonel with Captain Yamauchi
          we had brought
cigarettes cakes
          as it was lunch time
the Colonel said thank you in Japanese
          he ate with appetite
afterward he folded up his blanket and said:
          Please sit down
he asked us our names our rank our duties
          always smiling

          At the beginning
          the children were afraid
          but little by little
          they began to amuse themselves
          with Captain Yamauchi
          and the soldiers who were guarding them

* * *

Outside

                it was war
                inside
                it was very calm
                you'd have said another world
                Colonel Robert
                was uneasy
                he thought about his men
                perhaps wounded
                or dead

From the cavern

                you could hear
                the rifles in the town of Lang Son
                and the cannons of the Fort
                but within the cavern it was very calm
                you could almost believe in spring

* * *

On the 9th in the evening the Colonel
who had misplaced his kepi
asked me
to go to his home and find him another one
I was certain
that he was resigned to his death
on the 11th
I was not able to see him
on the 12th in the afternoon
I carried out the inspection as I did after every operation
and I went to see the Colonel
I greeted him
and he answered
he said good day to me in Japanese
he was alone
there were no guards
I don't know where the other prisoners were

* * *

When I entered
              he was reading his newspaper
then he calmly put it back in his closet
since we did not speak the same language
              we communicated our thoughts
              with gestures
              for quite a while

During the morning
              the other prisoners came back
              each one had gone back to his home
              accompanied by a soldier
to bring back clothing personal affairs

To have been in the Colonel's company
              made me happy
 he was waiting for death
              calmly
              sure of himself
—an honorable and holy deportment

* * *

How long did I stay there
            alone with him
I no longer remember
            as I was going
            I said goodbye to him
he took a few steps toward me smiling
just at the spot I indicated to you on the diagram
he said something that I didn't understand
perhaps it was
            Come and see me one day
            or Good-bye

Such a good man
a true hero
and we had to execute him
the next morning!

SUPERMAN, JOHNSON COUNTY, KENTUCKY.
PHOTOGRAPH BY GLORIA BAKER FEINSTEIN.

Two Poems

RICHARD JONES

The Darkness

That spring began with a catastrophe—
a baseball with the speed and force
of a cannonball struck me in the left eye.
My mother, called to the hospital,
saw the ruined face, her unconscious boy,
the blood-soaked T-shirt and jeans,
and believing I had been killed, fainted.
After the surgery, my father was told
there was a good chance I would lose
all sight in my left eye. I lay in bed
with my head and face wrapped
in gauze and bandages, fed with straws
and sleeping fitfully. Blind dreams
would spin my body on the mattress,
tangled and trapped in the white sheets,
until I had turned around, my head
at the foot of the bed. Each day,
an orderly would lift me in his arms.
To an eleven-year-old boy,
it was like flying or being raptured
while a chatty nurse changed the linens.
Then the orderly would gently
position me so that I rested properly
on the pillow, my body the hand of a clock
at midnight or noon, each hour the same.
Three weeks later, the family gathered
as the doctors unwrapped the bandages.
A pair of skilled hands lifted the gauze
in slow, careful circles from my eyes.
It must have been like a scene in a movie—

everyone held their breaths and asked
if I could see. I beheld a blue-yellow haze
and then figures, "like trees walking,"
as the blind man said in Mark's Gospel.
I recall that for a moment I did not speak.
A part of me, though young and untested,
knew something had been exchanged,
something purchased. The gift was mine.
My mother took my hand; my father wept.
The light was too much. I closed my eyes
and said to the listening darkness,
Do not be afraid. I see clearly.

The Shoeshine Box

My father passed it down,
the wooden shoeshine box
with the footstep on top.
I ask my grown son to sit
and allow me the honor
of polishing his boots.
He rests a foot on the step
as I kneel. We say nothing
as I dip my cloth in the wax
and start with the sides,
rubbing the heel and top,
the hard-to-get welt,
taking extra time to blacken
the sole, to polish the scars
and scratches. When all is
tuned up, as my father would say,
I sweep the brush back and forth,
the bristles making shushed music,
the redeemed shoe shining.
When you're gone, my son asks,
Can I have the wooden box?
Then he rises and strides forth
as my younger son takes a seat
and my daughter in the doorway
tells me she would be next.

Indianity

DIANE GLANCY

A form of Indianness that came from being on the margin.

At powwows when I saw girls dancing I was standing
still. I was not taken to powwows as a girl. I did not have
a shawl. I did not have turtle-shell leg-rattles. I did not
belong to the powwow not even knowing the powwow was
there. The words I impose on the page are my dancing.
As if the paper on which I wrote were a shawl sewn with
awl and bone-needle. Fragments of other fragments and
history scraped together. Girls dancing by desert tents.
On open plains. Grafted onto the land. A construct over
rough terrain.

Two Poems

E M I L Y   R A N S D E L L

Everywhere a River

I do remember darkness, how it snaked
through the alders, their ashen flanks
in our high-beams the color of stone.
That hollow slap as floodwater hit
the sides of the car. Was the radio on?
Had I been asleep?
Sometimes you have to tell a story
your entire life to get it right.

Twenty-two and terrified, I had married you
but barely knew you. And for forty years
I've told this story wrong. In my memory
you drove right through it, the river
already rising on the road behind us,
no turning around.
But since your illness I recall it
differently. Now that I know it's possible
to lose you, I'm finally remembering
it right. That night,
you threw that car in reverse,
and gunned it. You found us
another way home.

Leaving Ohio

—after Joe Millar

What did I lose along the highway
heading out of there,
gravel pits and pastures,
the slow gaze of cows,
the smell of pig iron and sulfur
in the wind.
Asphalt skies above foundries
and bean fields,
August heat pressing down.

Goodbye to guilt. To my father's
bones encased in lead.
Goodbye to his bucket list,
found in the drawer with his razor
after he died.

Goodbye to sweatshirts in the closet,
half-finished projects in the garage.
Memory hanging heavy
over everything here. The pioneer
gristmill and the towpath,
the Indian mound out by the golf course,
its purpose never unearthed,
the hundred shallow steps
I ran up each morning as my father
slept in his hospice bed.
Goodbye to the gods I prayed to
when I got to the top.

Our Distinguished Judges
The *New Letters* Awards for Writers

New Letters has been honored again, in this 35th year of the Literary Awards series, by the services of final judges who are prize-winning authors, gifted teachers, and astute critics.

 Fiction Judge Kevin Wilson is the author of two collections, *Tunneling to the Center of the Earth* (Ecco/Harper Perennial, 2009),which received an Alex Award from the American Library Association and the Shirley Jackson Award and *Baby You're Gonna BeMine* (Ecco, 2018); his three novels, include *Nothing to See Here* (Ecco, 2019). He is an associate professor in the English Department at Sewanee: The University of the South. Poetry Judge Gary Dop is  the author of the poetry collection *Father, Child, Water* (Red Hen P, 2015). His latest collection *Earth Never Settles* is forthcoming. He is the founding director of the M.F.A. in creative writing program at Randolph College in Lynchburg, Virginia, where he is an associate professor of English. Essay Judge Sheila Kohler is the author of 11 novels, three volumes of short fiction, a memoir, and many essays. Her most recent books include *Once We Were Sisters:*  *A Memoir* (Penguin, 2017) and *Open Secrets, a novel,* forthcoming from Penguin in 2020. She has won numerous prizes including an O.Henry Award and inclusion in *Best American Short Stories*. She has taught at Columbia, Sarah Lawrence, Bennington and Princeton. She lives in New York, New York.

All awards entries receive thorough and anonymous appraisal by our preliminary judges, themselves widely published writers. Our goal is to discover and promote great writing, and we receive entries from established writers along with new and under-recognized writers. Often, the new writers emerge, and we take a special delight in that.

Break Down Easy

TERRANCE MANNING JR.

In the spring of '98, my dad introduced my brothers and me to his buddy Steve, who had raced pro motocross in the '80s and early '90s. Dad said that if we were going to ride dirt bikes, we better do it right.

"Balls to the walls," Steve told us. "That's the only way to kick it, dudes."

It was sticky hot and sunny for May, and my brothers and I were sitting on an oily-black rail tie outside Dad's weld shop, where we'd been living for a year in a storage room behind the shop office. Sitting by the railroad tracks, we'd been instructed to keep our mouths shut, listen, and nod when Steve talked.

"You go big, or you go home," Steve said, pulling another line from his endless database of '90s gnarly-talk. He rattled them off like a preacher with prayer, and my brothers and I were eating it up.

We thought that Steve was rad. He rolled up in the passenger seat of Dad's truck, shirtless, smoking a cigarette, and when he stepped out, he was wearing these smooth '97 series comp-2 Fox boots, and black-and-white-striped Fox pants. He was cut up and skinny like a wrestler, and said *fuck yeah* and *yup* every couple of sentences.

Steve's RM250 was strapped down in the back of the truck, and after fifteen minutes of ride-it-wet philosophy lessons, he and Dad unloaded it.

When the engine started, I felt exhilarated by its scream, the way it roared when it revved, the way it rattled inside the frame—humming and impatient. Steve saddled it—no helmet, no shirt—and ripped across the gravel lot. He sped away, cut deep into turns, did some donuts, and sped right back, sliding rear-braked all the way up to where we stood with a tornado of dust swirling behind him. When he didn't quite stop in time, we had to dive out of the way, but all of us were laughing, cheering.

Dad burned down his cigarettes. He was smiling relentlessly. He even grabbed the bike from Steve and did a lap—though not as fast.

We took to the street, where Steve was going to talk to us about switching gears, when to pop or chop them, but he rode a wheelie down Juniper Street first, to show off for us. He started slowly, front tire lifting as he puttered in low RPM. He took one hand off and waved to us, and we clapped as he came in our direction, tire lifting higher. But as he passed, the bike was suddenly revving so loud and fast with the tire tilted so straight up that, in a sudden, horrifying second, the thing rocketed out from beneath him. Steve—at forty miles per hour—landed bare back to pavement, flipping, tumbling, and sliding nearly twenty feet before he crumpled up into a ball on the side of the road, and the bike crashed over the hillside.

I thought the dude was dead.

We sprinted toward him. The entire time, I was thinking no one could survive that. But, when we reached him, Steve stood up and said, "Took a gnarly spill, dudes," and we burst into laughter—part relieved, part amazed. Steve's back was skinned and bloody, and instead of calling it road rash, Dad kept laughing. *Got a new tattoo, man. Got a new tattoo.*

He loved it. And we did, too. Not lugging that heavy, gasoline-soaked bike back up over the hill, or watching blood ooze through mangled, gravelly skin, but the thrill of it all, and the danger. Though Steve's first lesson was getting broke on Juniper, we didn't see it that way. It wasn't reckless; it was fearless. Steve standing up laughing while he bled was tough, and that's what we'd learned to respect— that even broken, you don't break.

We'd only have to live at the shop, Dad told us, until his business took off. Once it became competitive with other machine and mechanical companies, he'd have enough money, finally, to find us a house.

Without the steady work, his crew was shrinking. Guys found jobs with better pay. Some quit. Some were fired. One guy stole Dad's Klein tools, replacing them with a bunch of knock-off, Harbor Freight wrenches, and when Dad figured it out, he went to the guy's house, where the guy was eating dinner with his family, and threatened to beat the hell out of him until the guy relented, walked Dad into the garage and gave back what he hadn't already sold.

Dad had one company left that hired him for everything: Arbor Dam, who developed hybrid vacuum systems for steam-system efficiency inside industrial plants and mills. They were his big fish, and he catered to them, even though it took everything—his money, his time. Even though the minute he finished a project, they shoveled up another.

Dad refused to slow down.

He picked up where his workers left off. When the painter quit, Dad strapped that scary-ass mask across his face and sprayed. When laborers quit, he cut and ground. He did layout and fab. He ran crane, picked up steel, and swept. He spent hours sand-blasting in the junk yard beside the shop, where a pile of sand, rust, and steel heaped like a dune among the wrecked cars. Then he'd work all night, even while we slept, bunched together on a mattress in the spare room of the office, his weld light blinking incessantly through the night, an electric blue lighting up the shop window. The noise was magnified by its closeness—welders, grinders—but we'd grown used to the sound, and other things: the hammering of steel; the blue light of the weld arc; the smell of rod flux burning off the sticks, and creeping thickly, slowly through the thin cracks around the room's door. We hung a blanket across the window to block the light and muffle the sound, but it only glowed, illuminating every stain and scrunched stitch or rip, and creating small, shapeless shadows that danced on the walls.

I want to say that's the reason I couldn't sleep—that all the noise, and the light, and the shadows kept me awake. But I'd started having a recurring nightmare, and sleep had become impossible.

Even now, I remember it: me on the top bunk of a bunkbed in a dark room, and from somewhere beneath, sharp, long-fingernailed hands scratch up the sides of the mattress, cutting and slashing for me. Outside a voice is calling. I used to think it was Dad's, the whiskey-throttle scratch in his throat as he talked, his quiet laugh. But I'm not sure anymore. I was always too struck with fear to move or yell for him, and when the room fell away, and those rabid fingers recoiled, there was only me on a mattress floating off to somewhere I didn't know, as if on a river. It was a sick feeling, like a fall dream, and it woke me. I had it so many times that I knew when I was in it. I hated, sometimes, to even sleep, for fear of feeling trapped, of being attacked, or alone, or floating off along some dark and silent river with a paralyzing terror that gutted me.

I could've told my dad, or my brothers, but I didn't want them to misinterpret my dream, or think that I was afraid of the dark; I wasn't.

I just couldn't sleep.

That summer, I'd begun to feel normal only in chaos, at the shop, with my brothers. While my friends crowded computers typing messages on AOL or played Mario Kart and Golden Eye in air-conditioned living rooms, we spent sunny days jumping trains, or climbing out under the train bridge with snacks and Turner's tea we'd stolen from Buy 'n' Fly. We ran barefoot beside the river, feet slapping in the sand and mud. We left pennies on the tracks for trains to flatten. We carved our names in trees with switchblades and flea-market penknives.

When Dad took the crew on site, he didn't return till dark. Since his truck had failed inspection, he'd leave it behind and ride with his guys. "Stay out of trouble," he'd smile. "I don't want to have to come home and kick ass." But my brothers and I knew he left his truck key in the gas cap, and we'd take the thing out and drive it around.

Chris was short, even for thirteen; he could hardly see over the wheel. But he was the oldest, so he was the driver. Jonny and I would climb into the bed, smiling when he gassed it. We laughed when he slammed the brakes and flung us forward, or zipped across the lot until, without slowing down, he sharply turned, sliding across the gravel and kicking up rocks. Sometimes, we pretended we were in the movies, like Nick Cage and John Travolta in *Face Off*, fist-fighting in a high-speed chase. Mostly, we collapsed on the bed floor so not to bounce out.

I remember feeling lost in those moments—everything swirling and draped in dust—belly laughing for fear. And when Chris skidded to a stop in the middle of the lot, we'd beg him, despite his objections, to do it again.

All of us were yearning for the same thing: excitement, if not a little danger. We fist-fought. We wrestled. We scaled the railroad for miles, where we held each in front of the train as it barreled toward us, until that moment before it reached us, when the horn moaned a desperate plea, and we'd dive from the tracks, laughing.

But all of that halted the day Dad promised—now that Steve was teaching us—that if we worked hard enough and became fast enough, he'd take us to the races to compete.

That's when everything changed, when all that chaos found a purpose, and making it to the races, suddenly, meant everything to us.

We still had the old putter-bucket, '81 XR, with the ripped-up seat, and broken pipe that made it sound like a muffler on wheels as we rode, but Dad had recently traded a welding machine with a guy for a '93 CR80. The thing had big, treaded wheels, a sleek red seat, and choppy graffiti graphics—a still shot of early-nineties extreme. Though it was probably too fast for us, Dad warned off the powerband, lifted Chris onto the seat, his toes barely reaching the ground, and said, "If you get scared, you jump off. Don't hang onto the damn thing."

Chris was clumsy at first. He popped the clutch, short-shifted, and wrecked a lot, but with some practice, and Steve's weekend lessons, he learned quickly.

Jonny was too scared to move. He rode slowly and fell over in the turns.

I, on the other hand, struggled with Dad's advice: *jump off when scared*. I held on—no matter how fast, or swirly, or out of control—because I used to think letting go meant admitting weakness.

When I slid off the seat, I wouldn't let go. I wrecked; I popped back up. I went over the bars; I took a breath and climbed back on.

I was determined, no matter how much it hurt, to be fast enough to race.

So, while Dad spent the summer beneath the perpetual darkness of his welding hood, my brothers and I rode up and down Juniper, getting used to speed. We did circles in the gravel. We climbed the hill beside the railroad, turned the bike around, and jumped back down. When the sun became relentless, we parked the bike and ran to the river. We crawled under the train bridge, thirty feet above the water, and hung out in the shade, imagining the races.

"So many people go to these things," Jonny told Chris and me the day Dad promised to take us. "Steve said they line the track, and they cheer so loud you can't hear the engine."

"If you're winning," Chris said. "Otherwise, they'll boo."

"We'll win," I said.

"No, I'll win," Chris said. "Jonny can be my mechanic. And T can . . . " he trailed off. "Well, T can lift my bike off the truck."

"Until you get tired," I said, laughing. "And *I* win. I'll be rich, and I'll steal Jonny from you. But don't worry, I'll give you money when you're older. Maybe even buy you a house."

"I want a truck," Jonny said. "An eighteen-wheeler with monster truck rims."

We threw things out more expensive and outlandish than the last—a ten-story building, a pet lion—each promising that if one of us made it, we'd never forget the others. We'd take care of them. We'd make them rich, too. And when the train roared over our heads, knocking hot rust onto our naked backs and into our eyes, we jumped off the bridge.

I doggy-paddled to the riverbank, where I could float around with my toes bouncing on and off the slick, muddy floor, while the boys drifted out toward the middle of the river.

"Let go of the rails," Chris yelled. "And learn how to swim, wimp." Dad's warning of the undertow—this uncontrollable and wicked current that I'd pictured as a giant toe that reached up and snatched little boys in the river—still frightened me. So, I drifted in the shallows until Chris and Jonny grew bored and swam back in.

"I can teach you," Chris told me on the walk back, "If you're scared or whatever."

"Teach me what?"

"To swim."

"I can swim," I said, scoffing. "I'm not afraid."

He rolled his eyes. "Suit yourself," and he laughed. "But you looked pretty scared hanging on the side of the river."

I was so pissed, I ignored him for the rest of the walk.

When we got back, I waited seething by the railroad for my turn with the bike. When it came, I didn't even tighten my helmet—something I'd taken to doing, a careless chic. I rode as fast and reckless as I could, because, with the bike beneath me and the engine rattling, it was a power I controlled; it was easy to be fearless, to fling from one side of the lot to the other until my turn was over, or we ran out of gas, or it became dusk, or my brothers and I were so tired from running and riding all day that we went inside afterwards and passed out on the pull-out mattress in the back room with sweat still wet on our skin, stinking, and sleeping deeply as we lumped beside each other in the dark.

At night, if I hadn't run myself into beautiful exhaustion, I was afraid to close my eyes and find myself trapped inside another nightmare. I'd lie listening to cranes drop metal at Tygart next door, or the Jake-break sputter of a truck tumbling down Rt.48, or car doors slamming in the parking lot as nightshift workers broke for lunch and ran outside to sleep across their back seats. Even Dad, who worked alone through the night, sounded like an entire crew outside the office window. He'd grind and torch and smack steel with a hammer to clean his welds, and the sound of the stick-welder—like a naked engine screaming on the floor—would ebb and flow in and out of high RPM with every pass. It had become a comfort to me, a feeling of closeness—him awake, him at work. All that sound inside my head was like a song. I could hear him pause to check his welds, the low idle humming almost quietly, and I'd wait, curled up inside those tiny moments for the noise to begin again, to rattle back to clamorous life and fill the room and the dark so that I could sleep, finally, without dreaming.

One night, there was a bang outside the window, and the welder shut all the way down. I heard Dad's hurried feet hustle toward the door, run inside, and jet to the bathroom.

"Damn," he growled.

I slipped off the bed, and into the beam of light just outside the bathroom door. "Hey," I said. "You all right?"

"Yeah, man," he said without looking, his head tilted to the side, his fingers searching. "Get back to bed, buddy." There was blood pouring out of his dark, sweaty hair. It was pooled stickily above his ear, dumping onto his cheek from a wide-open, jagged gash on his head. He'd sat up after a weld and rammed into the sharp edge of a pipe flange.

He must have noticed the shock on my face, or the fear, because he turned and said, "It looks worse than it feels, dude. I swear." Though he winced when he stuck his head in the sink and washed away the blood. He unraveled gauze and padded the wound. With his free hand, he pulled a bandana from his pocket and folded it in half, point to point, into a perfect triangle.

"Just have to cover it up," he said, slowly, as he draped the bandana over his head and tied a knot in the back. "I'm already behind." He looked in the mirror with a mug, pissed off and shaking his head. His beard was over-grown, sweaty, and black. His dark eyes looked darker with the deep-set sleeplessness that surrounded them.

"Does it hurt?"

"No," he said. "Not when you're a fuckin' rock." Then he looked at me and winked,

I just smiled and sat back on the bed, because that's what I believed, too: that Dad was invincible. He didn't hurt; he didn't break.

"When I finish this job," he whispered, kneeling next to the bed. "We'll be set, man. I promise."

"I know."

"We'll be out of here."

"I know."

"I found some houses. Big ones with big yards. We'll build a track. I can have a new shop. We'll be set."

"I know," I said again, because, if nothing else, we wanted the same thing: a house with a kitchen, a bathtub, and, hell yeah, a big yard—where my brothers and I could ride and race all day. I knew, too, maybe as much as I do now, that Dad was going all-in to take us there. The project he was working on was so large, he'd manufacture parts at the shop, then take his crew on-site to install them—piece by piece. I couldn't understand that pressure then, because I didn't understand money, or putting everything you make, and all that you have into a long-shot with a single payoff.

"I'm sorry I woke you," he said.

"I was awake."

"You all right?"

"Yeah," I said, because, right then, I was. Because if I told him I couldn't sleep, or that I was afraid to, he'd tell me not to worry, that he was ten feet away, and would whip anyone or anything that tried to hurt me.

So, I closed my eyes and pretended to sleep. I could feel him waiting in the doorway, in the dark, for a long time after that, watching. Then, he pulled the door shut with a click, and five minutes later, his welder crackled back to life.

One winter, when we lived in Highland Grove, the power company came and shut off our electric. I was five or six, but it wasn't unusual. One month, it was gas, and we wouldn't have hot water. Or it might be water, and we didn't shower. As long as we had fuel for the kerosene heaters—despite the thick stink of oil it left lingering—we'd be warm. And if the Kerosene ran dry, we'd lie in front of the open stove, holding our feet up to the heavy warmth that poured from its mouth. But that year, it was everything at once. No gas, so no stove. No Kerosene, so no heaters. No electric, so no anything. And Dad's arguments to the man—the kids in the house, the sick wife, and check he promised wouldn't bounce—elicited the same response: *I'm sorry; it's my job.*

Even when Dad threatened to fight him, the guy repeated his line and shut it all off.

The minute he left, Dad marched into the kitchen and told us, "They think they're smart." He stuffed tools into a brown-leather tool belt. "Watch Daddy out the window. We'll see who's fucking smart."

He'd done things like this before. He used a long metal key to turn the water back on at the street. He hooked an old meter up and diverted gas and water usage. He'd even been caught, threatened a couple times with heavy fines or jail time for "theft of services."

This was the first time I'd seen him climb the pole.

We watched him from the window in the living room. It was dark, the only light the flickering candles Mom had lit. It was so cold I could see Dad's labored breath as he tied his work boots, finished his beer, and burped, the splash of hot breath hitting the air like steam.

Mom was yelling for him to get back inside, but he climbed anyway, waving to us from the phone pole as he scaled it.

A few minutes later, the pole sparked at the wire, a firework that made a horrible electric croon when it burst, blowing Dad out into the air, then straight to the frozen ground.

He popped up as fast as he hit and started running toward the house.

My mom was screaming. My brothers and I were stunned. Dad was whipping his boots off, tearing gloves off his hands, and laughing his ass off as he slammed the door shut and locked it, afraid that someone might call the police. He waited awhile, then marched around the house pulling every blanket from the cupboards, every sheet from every bed, and every towel from the bathroom to cover us up.

We piled like puppies beneath the blankets in the bedroom, laughing and shivering until our bodies warmed, finally, to the bone, and we fell asleep.

In the morning, we had electric.

I'm not sure how, but I've always assumed Dad went out again once we were asleep and turned it back on.

At Dad's shop, he expected my brothers and me to behave the same way, believing, somehow, that we could bend the world, even beat it, with sheer relentlessness. And later, when we moved from the gravel shop lot to the trails beside the river, we did. We trained for the races. We put Steve's lessons to practice, called shit *gnarly*, and yelled, *Ewe yup*, and, *Fuck Yeah* to anything and everything. We built a whoops section, some tabletops and doubles. We cut turns around trees and across the creek.

In the middle of the trails was a hillside, forty or fifty feet tall. It was so steep, we couldn't climb it on foot without clawing fingernails into dirt or gripping roots and rocks to make it to the top. But, on the bikes, if we pinned the throttle, we could climb it in a single shot. That was my favorite part. Everything else took skill, but the hill was all guts. After we'd pooled at the top, we jumped back down, riding blindly off the cliff as if into nothing.

Sometimes, I'd ride off the edge so fast, I'd land near the bottom, to the point where, a few more feet, and my shocks would've sprung, or the bike or some tree could've crushed me. It was that line between having fun and being ruined that I loved so much, that thrilled me enough to do it time and again. Until, one day, when I was jumping back off, I collided with my friend, Bower, as he full-throttled for the top.

We smashed into each other, crunching.

My head smacked his engine. A light flashed. My arms ripped from the bars. My body spun. He landed at the top, where everyone watched, while I flipped down the hill with my bike.

I remember the silent, dizzy image of my friends and brothers sliding down after me. Their mouths were open, shouting, but I couldn't hear them. I hadn't realized that my helmet had broken off my head, or that it was lying in two pieces by the creek, or that my nose and lips were bleeding, and my elbows were skinned raw. When they reached me, I stood up, trying to shake off the ringing in my ears. "I'm fine," I told them, spitting a mouthful of blood. "Just took a gnarly spill."

And because they cheered for that, because I couldn't feel the gravelly, bleeding cuts on my arms, I felt, for the first time ever, like I was invincible.

But there's a difference between invincible and shock-numb, and as the adrenaline and fear wore off that night, and Dad started to clean my cuts in the shop bathroom, the raw ache of my bruised and cut-up body shook me back to reality.

At first, when I showed off the injuries to Dad, he laughed, asking if I liked my new tattoos. But he was pissed when he found out the helmet had broken, that the bike's bars were bent, and the clutch broken. Now, he was quiet as he took a bottle of peroxide and dumped it over my arms. It bubbled and foamed on my elbows as he picked gravel chunks from beneath the bloody skin.

I winced and jumped.

"Calm down," he said. "Bite back the pain." He scrubbed meticulously.

It hurt so bad, I could feel tears in my eyes. I clenched my teeth, pretending not to feel every jolt when the brush changed directions inside the cuts. I forgot to breathe. My face swelled and throbbed.

Dad stopped, looking angry. "What's the matter with you?" he asked, smacking me over the head.

"It's good," I said. "It's clean."

"I have to get the rocks out."

"It hurts."

"Quit moving," he yelled. "Sit straight. Be still. I'll get them out. You think you're the first dude to cut his arms?"

I tried not to cry, but I could feel it burning in my throat.

"You know," Dad said.   "You have to be willing, sometimes, to get hurt."

"I am."

"Then prove it."

But I didn't want to—especially not then.   Everything around me pulsed as my head ached and throbbed. My lips burned. My ears rang. I kept forgetting where I was. I felt like I'd been hit by a truck. I only wanted to sleep.

But Dad whacked me as I drifted off. "Prove it," he said again.

So, reluctantly, I stuck my arms out. I let him scrub until everything blurred—the pain, the conversation, the room— and sleepiness hit me, suddenly, like a drug.

When Dad finished, he wrapped my arms, lay me down, and told me, "That wasn't so bad, huh? You did good."

A few minutes later, I was asleep.

That night, and the weeks that followed, I was plagued with bad dreams: walls collapsing, teeth crumbling. Ones where I couldn't speak, couldn't punch, or was being chased by someone I couldn't see. I dreamt of lying in a room with no one around, everything floating away. It was always the same: being chased; suffocating; disappearing. I'm sure, now, that I had a concussion. But I wonder, sometimes, if the nightmares happened all at once, or all summer. If they were only after the wreck, or before, as I'd thought. It's difficult to recall that time without remembering those nights, or the inability to sleep that haunted me. It's hard to tell the difference between nightmares and dreams, because all of it is melded in my memory: the shop, the races, the chaos.

I know I dreamed. I've just forgotten them.

After a month of practice, Dad kept his promise. He took us to our first race: Pyramid Valley in West Virginia. Steve had found it, and was going to race, too—in A class—where he planned to make his return.

Dad bought a rusted-out three-rail trailer that looked like it had been wrecked and abandoned in a field for years. He welded the cracks, cleaned the rust, and though it still looked ugly, he latched it to the pickup. We loaded the CR into the truck bed, and strapped Steve's RM down on the trailer.

"Get ready to kick some ass," Dad told us on the drive. "They won't know what hit 'em."

"Yup," Steve said, his arm out the window, hand surf-boarding the wind. "You dudes are ready."

We rolled into the races hooting, hollering, ripping rebel yells out the front window as we bumped and rattled through the field to find a place to park. There were Winnebagos all over, pop-up tents sprung like trees, and lawn furniture along the track. I'd imagined there'd be stands, or bleachers, but there was only a low, wooden fence separating the track from the grass, where people were standing, or sitting on coolers, drinking beers.

Dad found a space near the concessions stands, where a row of people with lifted trucks, SUVs, and long-bed trailers were already parked, their new bikes on display, the latest models of every brand: '97 and '98 RMs, YZs, KXs and CRs— hoisted up on stands and glistening in the sun.

We stuck out beside them.

Dad backed the three-rail up to the woods line, and we unloaded the Styrofoam cooler, the old bikes. A kid next to us yelled, "Sweet rides," with a big smile on his face, then ran laughing into his trailer.

But we didn't care—that we were sharing a bike, that Dad's truck was beat to shit, or that all the rubber we brought was worn-down and bald—because all that time Steve had trained us, all that time on the gravel track, or down the trails, or finding gears on Juniper; all those wrecks, those broken clutches, broken levers, bruised and bloodied skin, we were the ones who put in the work. We couldn't wait to beat the snot out of the snobs—which is what Dad called them: *sissy snobs*.   He said that while they were sleeping in AC, with their fluffy pillows and silk socks, my brothers and I were training for the fight. And we liked that, because we couldn't wait to race and win. We couldn't wait to send them riding home crying in their fancy trucks and trailers.

So, we ran to registration, laughing. We chased each other along the side of the track, rooting for people who we didn't know.

We were the hungry ones. *We* were ready.

Until, when it came time for us to race, *we* got our asses kicked—all of us. Even Steve, who, once he was too far behind, pulled off the track.

Chris fell in the corners. I jumped the gate. We broke the number plate off the bike. At one point, our motoes were so close, I waited on the side of the track with a gas can for Chris to finish his race, so I could fill the tank and get straight to the starting line.

We were embarrassed and stunned by the precision, speed, and skill of other riders. They weren't wimps like Dad had promised, and they made us look like goons.

Those kids we parked near, who we'd smiled at when they mocked our bikes, were rebel yelling, now, from their windows as they left—the way we'd done when we arrived. We just loaded up the broken, over-heated bikes. I couldn't bring myself to look up and see their faces.

On the way home, Chris and Jonny slept in the bed of the truck, curled up beside the empty gas cans and muddy tires of the CR. I sat up front, squeezed between Dad and Steve. Neither offered advice. Steve slept, and Dad smoked while the sun went down ahead of us. I remember being pissed at Dad. When he tried to talk, I'd pretend to sleep. I can see him still, one arm out the window, a cigarette in his hand, the other bumping the radio up in tiny increments. I remember the warm, summer air rushing in with the smell of smoke and sweat and two-stoke exhaust, the sound of George Straight's "One Night at A Time" on the radio. Dad singing. It embarrasses me, now, that I was pissed at him then, because I realize he wasn't trying to keep us busy. He wasn't feeding the insatiable, teenaged craving for adrenaline and speed we'd already started to chase. He was trying to give us something to make us feel better than we were. He wanted us to feel like kids—normal kids—since living in his weld shop, and showering under a hose, and passing time on the tracks or in a junk yard or exploring an industrial park wasn't normal; bikes were. Training for the races made us feel like we were in control of it all. The prospect of winning gave us a secret feeling of hope, as if, somehow, we might be able to race our way out.

But I imagine, now, it must have felt like it backfired on him.

After Pyramid Valley, Dad got serious about the bike. He wanted to learn everything he could about the engine, or jets, or suspension.

This is what I noticed: Dad on the practice track timing us. Dad tweaking the bike. Dad demanding that we get faster if we expected, ever, to win. Dad telling us, "It's not over. You win, and you lose. That's the way it is. But you won't get nothing if you break down easy."

This is what I didn't notice: the big rigs stop showing up. Dad's workers working their way to new jobs. Dad's tools along the walls, greasy and unused. The sand-blast pile washing slowly away in the junkyard until there was nothing left but a flat beach of toxic, rained-out sand. I didn't know that Dad's big fish had gotten away, had gone out of business. That that project Dad was working on, the tank that he'd built in pieces, that he'd constructed on site, and sunk everything into—man hours, money, and hope— was suddenly worthless. That even after court, they paid pennies on the dollar.

It was a moment for Dad's company where it wasn't over yet but had reached a point where it was impossible to recover.

I only knew then that Dad still welded in the shop, that my brothers and I still practiced. It was like reflex for us, our bodies in motion: we kept moving, kept working, and expecting, still, that the big win was coming.

Instead, at the end of July, something else happened. On our way back from the trails one day, we passed these truckers parked in front of Markers—the business across the lot.

Steve and Jonny were out front, and Chris and I were in the back. The guys were standing around their rigs.

Chris, showing off, slowed down and did a donut, flinging me off the back of the bike. Chris saw the truckers laughing as I climbed back on, and he flicked them off. Then he rode up close, slammed the throttle, and roosted them with a machine-gun fire of gravel and dirt from the back tire.

They immediately started chasing us, screaming. They threw rocks at us. I was laughing until one hit me in the back so hard it took my breath away.

We flew into the shop doors, where Dad was standing with Jonny and Steve.

The truckers were making their way across the lot behind us. There was a group, maybe three or four, and when Dad asked what their problem was, we told the truth: Chris was playing around; he roosted their trucks; they threw the rocks. "But it doesn't hurt anymore," I said. "It doesn't even matter."

"The hell it doesn't," Dad said, before he jogged out to meet the men in the middle of the lot, already shouting.

I almost felt sorry for the truckers, imagining how bad Dad was about to kick their asses. Until one guy, who'd drug a bat out with him, started swinging it. And everyone, suddenly, was punching. Dad charged the group, bear-hugging his way to the ground as they piled onto him—kicking. The guy with the bat swung it relentlessly. The sound of it—the muffled, wooden thud—boomed across the lot.

I thought that they were going to beat him to death.

Even now, it amazes me. That I stood there watching.
That Steve, who didn't run out to help, convinced us to,
"Stay cool, dudes; he's got this," because, I think, that's
what we all believed. And it amazes me that Chris managed
to sneak inside and call Dad's friend, Jimmy, who worked up
the street. Or that Jimmy made it there so quickly, blasting
into the lot with gravel and dust swirling around his truck
like a storm. That before he got there, Dad wasn't getting
up; he wasn't winning. That it surprised me, still, that he
wasn't invincible.

When Jimmy reached them, the truckers scattered. But
Jimmy and some others jumped out and blocked them.

Someone pulled a knife.

"Get inside," Steve told us, finally, when police lights
flickered from the street above, and the sound of sirens
echoed in the distance. "Get in the shop."

Inside, I could hear cars pouring into the lot. Voices
shouting. Doors slamming. As dusk settled over the
shop, police lights cut up the darkness with their blinking,
incessant red glow, and I wondered if someone had been
killed. But a little while later, as cars drove slowly back
off the lot, Dad, Jimmy, and the others came bumping and
yelling into the dark office.

"Jesus," Jimmy said. "Are the boys hiding in here?" All
of them burst into laughter, which, as we crawled from the
darkness of the back room, made me feel stupid.

They turned on the lights and I could see Dad's face
was blasted. His eyes were dark and swollen. His nose was
bent. His lips were bloody. He had a cut on his temple, and
visible lumps on his arms and head from where he'd warded
off blows from the bat.

It shook me.

Not the blood, or the cuts, but his pained and hollow
laugh as they recapped what had happened: how Dad had

known the cops; how no one wanted to press charges, because, the police said, it was a "mutual combat" between idiots, whose punishment was immediate and visible. No one was killed, and Jimmy's buddy, who had pulled the knife and threatened to gut anyone who moved while Dad got up from the ground, had thrown the thing across the railroad when the police came. He spent the evening in the dark looking for it.

I could tell Dad couldn't wait for them to leave. He was slumped in an office chair, drinking a beer and hardly talking. But he let them stay and drink, too. He ordered pizza.

And later, once the pizzas were finished, and stories of what happened told and retold, Jimmy and his buddies left, and the chaos calmed. Dad lay on the couch in the storage room. He didn't pull out the bed. He couldn't. He was fucked up, he said. He could hardly walk, could hardly breath. He only wanted to rest.

Then, after a few minutes, he fell asleep with one arm thrown over his eyes, his bruised and broken hand hanging limply by his ear.

My brothers and I spread a sheet on the storage-room floor, just in front of the couch, where Dad lay swollen and moaning.

It was so hot, all of us were in underwear, and a box fan blew heavily from the corner of the room. I'm sure Chris and Jonny were feeling what I felt, too: guilty, even shocked. I was too afraid to ask. I was too afraid to speak. My hands were trembling. My chest hurt. I couldn't calm down—no matter how much pizza we'd eaten, or how hard we laughed about Dad getting his ass kicked with a bat.

Instead, I lay in the dark feeling like crying. From the hot summer night, maybe. Or the box fan's ceaseless clunk and rattle. Or Dad snoring so loudly. Or my brothers snoring so softly, so quickly. Or, maybe, from the fear I felt: of sleeping, of dreaming, of finding myself lost in another of the endless nightmares of those nights, or my life, where I was afraid, always, of losing; or being trapped, or disappearing into insignificance; of an inability to be strong enough, or tough; of never being better than what I was—this river boy, poor boy, loser; of Dad, and all his rage; of Dad, and his promises.

I lay on the concrete floor like a fool, waiting, still, for the fruits of his lessons: fight at all costs, and be loyal to each other. Maybe that way, we wouldn't be crushed beneath the weight of the world.

The last week of August, a few weeks after Dad fought the truckers, Chris and Jonny convinced me to wade away from the river's edge and swim across the Youghiogheny.

Chris had done it once already, and, now, he wanted us to swim it with him.

So, he gave us the same five-minute lessons Dad had given all of us: how to breaststroke, how to backstroke if we grew tired, lessons my brothers picked up the first time, where I, the bigger and clumsier of the three, had only pretended to understand.

"If you're having trouble," Chris said, "just yell." Then we took off across the river.

But, half way out, I freaked.

Already winded, the other side seemed so suddenly impossible to reach. I panicked. I doggy paddled—which was worthless in the current.

Chris sent Jonny across and swam back for me. I fought him off at first, claiming angrily that I could do it, that I could make it. "Just chill," he said. "Take a breath and hold it. You'll float."

So, I took it.

And right then, he scooped his arms beneath mine, tilting my face toward the sky, and swam backwards. I stopped fighting and floated on my back, holding wind in my chest, while Chris swam.

I remember him talking the entire time. *Calm down, buddy. We're good. We're almost there, I promise*—never yelling, or letting go, or making me feel stupid for being frightened. Instead, he said, "I was scared, too, the first time I swam it. But after this, it's easy."

Something I took as a promise: *after this*, it's easy; because, *after this,* we win.

And after *this*, Chris was nearly right, his promise nearly prophetic. That summer, he won his first race. Then another, and another, and everything is easy when you've got something to hope for—like the prospect of him becoming a child athlete, or small-town success story, or, we all thought, the one who'd carve our way out. Even the next winter we spent at the shop, the worst one, where Dad was broke, the business gone, and food disappeared, Dad sold off his welders, his torches, his sandblasters, plasmas, and painters to get Chris a good bike with a good engine so he could compete and win and carry us where Dad couldn't.

Everything is easy when you believe a change is coming.

Even now, I go back to this summer, and this day on the river, because it's the last time I truly believed in that notion. It's before Dad packed us into his truck with nothing but our bed, our clothes, and the bike, looking for anywhere to stay a few nights or weeks at a time, until Chris got a factory ride, or went pro, and all of our problems would be over. Before Chris ripped his knee two years later and ended that dream. Before Dad fell heavily into drinking, or we spent the next six years waiting, still, for something to change. Before Chris became addicted to his pain pills, and Jonny joined him, and eventually, the two of them found heroine. Before the only one to ever make it out, to find a life with some stability, even love, was me—at the cost of leaving all of them, and the dreams we dreamed, inside the memory of those years. Because no one is tough enough, or fearless enough, to bend the world to their will.

But that day in the water, we believed we could. We hadn't won yet, but we hadn't lost either. And we didn't fight the river's current—that dark, powerful undertow. We let its muddy water carry us down river, where, far from where we started, we reached the other side. Jonny had run the whole way watching over us, cheering from the riverbanks, calling out the rocky spots, and places we could land or crawl up. When we made it to the shallow edge, Chris let me go. I faced him a moment as he floated there, laughing as he splashed river water lightly with his hands and looked deep into the Mon Valley. Then I turned and swam, racing toward where Jonny jogged along the bank, wading himself through water and stone, smiling and clapping as the sunlight beat down on his tiny pale chest.

I'd be there, too, in a moment.

Two Poems

BRIANNA FLAVIN

Grape Tomatoes

Then each morning, tumbling planets
of warm, beating juice palpable
in each small womb. They split
their skins when I come round,
piling into caviar in my clothes.
How gory I look,
slimed with seeds
the blood smelling sweet on me,
my knife fisted, my grip sure
and every sweaty hair gathering
dirt. It cakes into my scrapes,
balms the burns—this soil
wards the stinging bugs
better than a shirt. If you saw me
now, you would not say *sweetheart*
or if you did, you'd mean
the gallons of grape tomatoes
gathered against me
in a hundred hearts, flaring
like a hive of bees, and yeah
they're pretty sweet, but you
would not say *mommy*
like a saccharine Hallmark
greeting, like something
you could sneer at or dismiss
if you saw me like this.

Orion

Smoke obscures her vision
of Orion, the rising dot, dot, dot
over our campfire spread around with quilts
patched purple, maroon and gold, wine spills
all camouflaged, and she can spill still more.
Frogs chirp from the creek and the grapevines
of her backyard where the neighborhood gathers.
Firebread, moss-green bottles, her fingerspell
on nylon strings. Those folk songs
used to earn something in bars when my dad
was a boy, and now her wild, white head bends over
the acoustic, eyes gleamy as the stream they found
her second husband, Jerry, by,
the man she truly loved—with his face to the sky,
just as she saw by dream.
I'm drifting in and out of smoke
and sleep, listening to her voice
lowlit as sedge grass with sun in it, faces of uncles
and the neighbor Sylvia, some local
kids all murmuring in a glow
spattered with sparks while the breadsticks
cook slow. My sisters' heads next to mine
on the blanket, smeared with marshmallow
and ash, closing our eyes
every time her voice comes back, azimuth
strung taut as a guitar string, linking us
to elsewhere, as though Jerry's time and ours
could overlap, two currents in a rhythm,
two tellings of a tale, as though face
to the stars we could draw our own lines
and spell out the symbol we wanted, write it
over our people.

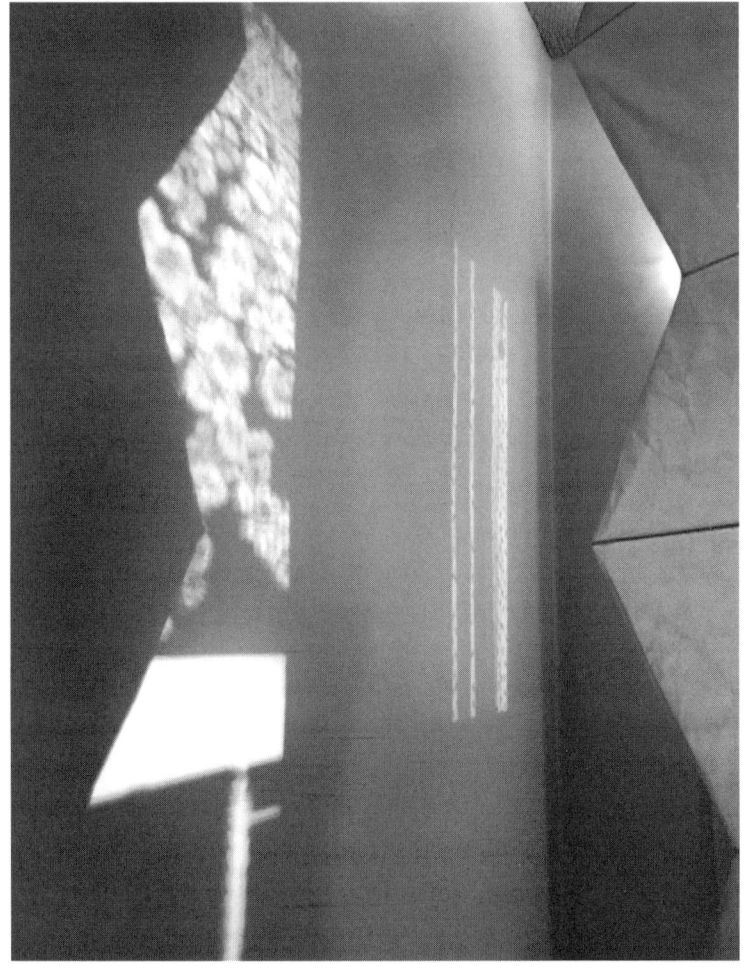

ABSTRACTION.
PHOTOGRAPH BY REBECCA OFIESH.

Jessica touches my guts

ANGIE SIJUN LOU

Jessica puts her fingers all the way inside me like she is reaching up to hold my guts. I'm lying sideways on the bed with my underwear around my ankles, trying to stay cool about this. Her nails are sparkly and manicured to perfect points, like diamonds cut rough at the tip of her fingers.

—Can you feel it? It's two plastic strings.

—I can't tell. I don't think I'm deep enough.

—You can't go any deeper. You'll be in my ribcage.

I reach to grab her wrist but she pushes my hand away.

—You've got to stop writhing around. Just hold still.

I try to meditate on the ceiling fan that whirls above us, the concentric circles it traces in its path. It's the dead of winter but I can't turn it off because the chain is broken, so my skin rises in goosebumps under its gaze. I run my hands over my belly, imagining the metal hook of my IUD lost somewhere inside me, maybe in my intestines or all the way up in my liver. Jessica shakes her bangs away from her face. The pressure from her fingers pushes up into my belly, blunt and relentless, until it feels like her entire hand has disappeared inside me.

—I think I feel something.

—Is it hard and plastic?

—It doesn't feel like everything else.

—Are there two of them?

She digs around some more against my cervix.

—Yes.

—That's it. That's my IUD.

She takes her fingers all the way out and looks at me.

—So it's not dislodged. You're fine.

She gets up and goes to the bathroom to wash her hands, and as soon as I hear the water running cool and blue, my stomachache goes away. Today I ate meat for the first time in over a decade, and afterward I felt a sharp pain inside me that I imagined was my IUD being ejected out of my body. I made Jessica leave the party because it hurt so bad. I clutched my stomach like it was a wounded animal and interrupted her while she was kissing some girl on the dance floor. It's ok, she said, I hate this party; let's go home. When we got home I still couldn't find it, not even when I squatted down low on the bathroom tiles and reached inside me, and that's when I started freaking out.

Jessica comes back with a white pill and a glass of water.

—Eat this ibuprofen.

I swallow it and drink the water so fast I come up gasping for air. I look at her sheepishly.

—I'm sorry I made you do that. I think it's the meat we ate earlier, it's giving me a stomachache. I thought I felt something sharp poking from the inside.

She takes her earrings out and throws them on the floor.

—It's ok. Just another bonding activity, you know. Can I sleep in your bed? I forgot to hang my sheets up to dry.

She doesn't wait for an answer before she turns off the lights. In the murky darkness I can see the outline of her plants on my windowsill, how the leaves droop low and graze the soil it's rooted in. I dip my fingers in the dirt and it's soaking wet. She put her plants in my room so they can get more sunlight, but I don't think that's why they're dying. I haven't told Jessica she's over watering them, and if I did she still wouldn't stop.

Jessica lets out a faint sigh before she gets hooked in a heavy dream. I feel hyper aware of her body lying next to mine so I try to separate myself, but I end up squished in a corner while the ceiling fan blows her long black hair all over my face.

The reason why I haven't eaten meat in over a decade is because I accidentally killed a pool of frogs when I was 12 years old. I had just spent the summer making a pond in my backyard, and I poured my adolescent heart into it—I pulled wild grass from its roots, hollowed out the black earth, laid down a tarp, planted lily pads, filled it with water, and set all the frogs from PetSmart free.

In September there was a long drought in California. The television told us you could get a fine just for watering your lawn. Frogs croak loudest before the rain, but it had been days since I had heard a single sound. This is why I waited until nightfall, when nobody was looking, and secretly poured cups of water into the pond, wanting to submerge the frogs as deep as possible so they wouldn't get pierced by the light.

But in the mornings the sun was the heaviest. It weighed down the whole sky. I was the first person to see that the frogs had been scorched by it. I learned that water refracts light, acting as a kind of lens, and this makes the sunlight focus in intense patches, causing small, localized burns. This is what my father told me after I went outside and saw the frogs burnt to crisps: their bodies floated belly-up to the surface, arms and legs splayed wide, and in that moment I knew I would never eat meat again.

I told Jessica this story while we were chatting at a Chinese restaurant inside a strip mall, half-joking and half-not. I showed her my bare hands and emphasized that I had used them to commit a special kind of slaughter. She rolled her eyes and called the waitress over, speaking to her in Shanghainese so I couldn't understand.

When the waitress brought a steaming plate of fried frog legs doused in chili sauce, I sat there frozen with my eyes wide while Jessica laughed hysterically. I couldn't believe I had told her my secret and she was making me relive it now, years later, after the memory of meat had long dissipated. She ripped off one leg and held it up to my mouth. Trust me for once, she said. I parted my lips and took a bite, chewing slowly, tasting the muscles glazed in oil. As soon as we left the restaurant my belly started hurting, and I knew it was the frog legs kicking inside me.

For weeks after the frogs were fried to death, my father mowed the lawn and the ones who had escaped from the pond alive would get stuck in the blades. He always cut the power and crouched down low to rescue them, balancing a frog with one severed leg in the palm of his hand.

I know you shouldn't have a crush on someone you live with but these things are inevitable. It started the first time I pulled up to the house and saw Jessica standing there in camouflage Dickies, leaning on her pink Pepto-Dismal colored truck parked in the long driveway. I had e-mailed her on Craigslist earlier that week before driving my rental van down the coast. The images were blurry and the house was trashed and everything in the listing was spelled wrong. Cheapest rent in east L.A., it said. And that was enough for me.

When she helped me unload my moving van, I became fixated on the way her elbows looked with the sleeves rolled up, the drops of sweat sliding down her limbs. They were so smooth I felt like she could put her entire arm inside me and it still wouldn't hurt. My uncle in Shanghai signed a lease on this place so his wife could have her baby here, she said.

So the kid would have citizenship, or whatever. She flicked her wrist and I heard it crack.

When she finally reached up inside me, it did hurt a lot. Only because I wanted the touch to signify something but instead it was so banal. There is a myth from the Han dynasty my grandmother used to tell me, about a spirit girl who gets reincarnated as a real girl—she's from another world that's parallel to this one, but it's virtual and inaccessible. On her wedding night, she sits on her bridal bed and waits for her husband to come take her virginity. The moment he reaches for her, she says, "Wait, I'm still ethereal." Meaning: wait, you can't go inside me yet. I'm not completely *here*.

When her hand slipped inside me, I felt her carving out a vacancy where my body used to be: here is a hand, and here is a void.

———————

The morning after Jessica puts her entire hand inside me happens to be her mom's birthday. She would have been 44 this year. Jessica says 44 is unlucky because it has the number four twice, and the number four has the same Pinyin as death. 四 sounds just like 死 if you don't listen closely. This is why there is no fourth floor in most buildings in China—the floors on the elevators skip straight from three to five.

Jessica explains this to me in the parking lot of a gas station where we stopped to buy wasabi peas and incense.

—Your parents never told you this?

—No, never.

—They aren't superstitious?

—They are. But only when they want me to behave. They say every grain of rice I leave in the bowl will grow to become a pimple on my lover's face.

She starts the engine and whips a U-turn.

—My mom used to say that, too. She wouldn't let me leave the table unless I'd eaten every single grain.

I roll my eyes.

—I hate that. I would never make my kids do that.

Jessica opens the bag of wasabi peas and pours some in her mouth.

—I don't know. Maybe I would.

Jessica needs incense because she wants to make a shrine in our living room for her dead mother. She's decorating the shrine with incense and a lock of hair. Over time she says she'll add things like a keychain of Guanyin, or a letter she wrote and never sent, or a grapefruit peeled all at once so the skin hangs off long and coiling. I promised Jessica I'd participate in a ritual she's performing in her honor, but she won't tell me anything about it.

—So who taught you this ritual?

—Nobody.

—You looked it up on the Internet?

She shakes her head.

Jessica threw out her uncle's couch last week, and when I came home from work someone had already taken it from the street. This is the perfect place for a shrine, she said, gesturing at all the emptiness. This made me angry, but not angry enough to get a new couch. Now every evening we watch television sitting on the floor, slurping bowls of instant ramen with our legs sprawled out in front of us.

When we get home from the gas station, Jessica fixes our broken printer by hitting it, over and over, until it spits out a photo of her mother sitting on the hood of a minivan in the summer. Her hair is tousled gently by the ocean behind her, and she has her hands cupped around a cigarette as she tries to light it.

—She's pretty.

—A real babe, right?

—You have her mouth.

She blows on the photo to dry the ink, spitting everywhere.

—She gave me her mouth and her bad temper and that's it.

Jessica leaves the room like someone who will be right back. From the bathroom she yells at me to turn the smoke detector off, so I step on a chair and stab it with the broom, catching the batteries in my hand as they fall out of the sky. When Jessica comes back she's wearing a *qipao* that's too tight, with the top buttons undone.

—This is my mom's wedding dress.

She sucks her belly in and stands up straight.

—It's nice. I like the red silk.

—Thank you.

She leans over and her breasts spill out.

On the ash-stained carpet of the living room, Jessica pushes sticks of incense into a rotting apple, making puncture wounds with her nails, leaving claw marks all over it. Her mom is a digital mirage taped on the altar, too real and not real enough. Jessica goes to the kitchen and arranges some pork buns on a plate.

—Here.

She hands me a bun.

—No, thank you.

—Take it. It's part of the ritual.

—I don't eat meat.

She flops the bun into my lap. I look at her.

—I thought you were making this up along the way.

—I am, and this is what I've decided to do. We have to share a meal with the dead.

She takes another from the plate and bites into it.

I touch the bun's pillowy texture between my fingers and kneel beside her, bathed in incense smoke. I watch her hold the incense up to her forehead before pressing her face to the carpet in prayer. She rises and repeats this three more times. I want to perform the ritual exactly as instructed, so I mirror Jessica and bite into my bun slowly, deliberately, trying to forget that what's in my mouth was once an animal. As soon as I taste the salt crystals buried between the folds of flesh, my instinct is to spit it out. It takes all my love for Jessica to close my eyes and swallow instead.

Once, when I was on LSD at a warehouse show, I witnessed a woman eating a hot dog on the dance floor by squirting streams of ketchup straight into her mouth. The lights above us shined neon and bright, forcing the hot dog to have a subtle metallic sheen. I couldn't look away, even after the hot dog had long disappeared inside of her, and there was no sign of its existence except a smear of ketchup on her upper lip, a scarlet brand.

This reinforced my stance on meat because I don't like how a living thing can be swallowed so seamlessly. The act of consuming meat becomes a transgression where the other being is disappeared without a trace, but there is no prior relationship before the act of consummation. It's almost as if the telos of the animal is to be ingested by me. I don't understand which bodies are worth being mourned and which ones aren't. I told this to Jessica and she rolled her eyes and said I shouldn't eat plants either because they have feelings, too. They grow more if you play classical music and speak softly in their presence. Plants that live in houses where everybody screams and throw dishes at each other don't grow at all. Jessica knows this for a fact.

I think about the color red. If I could wear red every day, I would, but it doesn't go well with my dark complexion so I wear it sparingly, in splashes, at dim parties where only I know it's there. You can see the redness of meat when it's pressed against the blue ice of the supermarket, its icy tendrils sprouting under the clear Saran Wrap—

Red is the color of Jessica's *qipao* flashing in the dark. She spins around and around in circles, eating slices of grapefruit taken from her mom's altar, the red juice dribbling down her chin.

Jessica spends more time on the phone than anyone I've ever met. All day long she sits hunched over the receiver with the volume turned up so it drowns out the white noise from the freeway. When she speaks to her cousins in Chinese it always sounds like she's trying to start a fight. Each vowel comes out quick and oceanic. I could never move my tongue that fast without choking on it, but in our water-streaked mirror I watch myself try.

When Jessica talks to her clients she speaks in a bored, sultry voice. She gets the most requests on Monday nights, when husbands have been with their wives and kids all weekend, and are ready to let go of their rage. She hangs up their calls without saying goodbye. Chinese people don't say bye, she explains. They say, uh, uhh, and hang up. I practice when she's gone. Uh, uhh, and I slam the phone back on the hook and storm out of the room.

Once I witnessed her painting her nails and chatting on the phone with the cord tangled around her fingers, long and wild like a snake. She doesn't turn the lights on to save electricity. There was a bright pink stain on the back of her hand, like a scythe glinting in the dark. After she hung up, I pointed at her hand and asked, what's that. She told me she was just blotting her lip gloss, but she hesitated for a moment, so I knew she was using the back of her hand to practice kissing.

I couldn't figure out why someone like Jessica would need all that practice. After she went to work I spent a long time with the back of my own hand, coating it with spit, nibbling my flesh to get the full effect. I wondered who Jessica was thinking about—maybe the pretty rave girl from last weekend, or the bartender with the cargo pants and teardrop tattoo, etc. I kissed myself and thought about Jessica's public and private fantasies, wondering if there was a place for me inside them.

———————————

Later at night I watch television alone until my eyes sting from the light, waiting for enough time to pass before I can visit Jessica at work without seeming desperate. She told me to come early before it gets busy, but I wanted to wait longer so she could have some space to miss me.

As the clock strikes eleven, I get in my car. I spend an hour in traffic with my fog lights on, and when I finally pull up to the Déjà Vu at Union Station it's close to midnight. Since the train only comes once an hour, all the men are inside the club, drinking whiskey and killing time. I push open the swinging doors and the first thing I see is Jessica on stage, dancing on a pole, her body twisting and untwisting against the metal bar. I think about the way fish look when they are thrashing upstream to spawn, searching for the precise location where they first hatched.

My grandmother told me a story once about the fish in the village where she grew up, how nobody was allowed to eat them because their souls were too big for their bodies. Anyone could eat large cattle (cows, horses, bison), but the consumption of small creatures was ritually forbidden because the amount of meat they produce isn't enough to justify their killing. There is an economy between the soul and the hunger it satiates—when Jessica's flesh presses against the pole, I know she could feed everyone in the room except for me.

The men wave dollar bills in the air and don't give them up unless she moves real close to them. I don't know what to do with my hands, so I go to the bar and order a drink. I take a faraway booth to try to act cool and disinterested, biting my straw while Jessica works the floor in her sky-high heels. I keep squinting to find her scar in the dark.

Jessica has a forehead scar from drowning in the deep end of a swimming pool when she was 14 years old. It happened when she first moved to America, and to this day she is afraid of large bodies of water. It's a deep cut that splits her forehead diagonally, in half, which she hides underneath a thick layer of foundation and cropped bangs. I guess the scar throbs whenever it's about to rain because it can detect moisture in the air. It's why I can never leave

L.A., she says, most other cities make my face hurt. But in the club light I can't see it at all—it's like the scar has disappeared, or maybe it's healed over.

An older man walks up to her and hands her a bill. He leans in to whisper something, and she flips her hair and walks away. He keeps following her down the platform even after she's turned her back to him. I don't know why, but I can feel my palms clench and unclench in my lap. When he reaches out to untie her G-string, that's when I slam my drink on the table, spilling most of it on my hoodie. It makes a stain the shape of a halo across my chest.

I walk over and grab his shoulder.

—What are you doing?

He waves the bill in the air.

—Nothing, sweetie. I'm just giving her a tip.

He looks me up and down.

—Are you the bouncer?

He smiles. I can see his braces glinting in the dark.

—I saw what you were doing. Don't touch her.

—Calm down, I'm not touching her, I'm just paying her.

I slap him across the face. Before I can lunge for him, I feel the actual bouncer's hand on my shoulder, so I spit on the man's shirt one last time before I get taken away.

A few minutes later, Jessica comes outside to find me sitting on the curb with my hood over my face, fuming mad. She can't stop laughing for some reason. Men, she says, are all like that.

—I was just teasing him because he's a regular and he just got paid today. You don't need to get so worked up. How come you're all wet?

—I spilled my drink.

—Come back inside, let's get you cleaned up.

She grabs on my arm and I move her hand away.

—Please leave me alone.

She pulls on the strings on my hoodie until she's nearly choking me, laughing as my face becomes scrunched up.

—Stop!

—You know, that guy back there, Mr. Calcagni, he used to be my history teacher.

I cough up some spit onto the street to seem tough.

—Yeah? You let your history teacher feel you up like that?

She snaps her gum at me.

—He's not my teacher anymore.

She sits down and drapes her legs over mine.

—Listen, everything's fine. I know you want to look after me, but everything's fine.

She puts her head on my shoulder. I think about why someone that old would still choose to get braces. He must be a psychopath.

—I just don't like when I see someone touching you.

—He wasn't fucking with me. He was paying me. Come on, I'm done for the night.

—You're not going back in?

—I'm hungry. I want to go to McDonald's before it closes.

She runs her fingers over her scar.

—I don't know why it hurts so bad right now.

We both look up at the cloudless sky and that's when I start laughing, too.

At the drive-thru Jessica teaches me weird things she says in Chinese to get more tips when she's dancing. 买一块鸡肉撞死你, she says. That means I want to beat you to death with a chicken nugget, and then she bites down on one. Nobody in this part of town speaks Chinese, even though a lot of people have Chinese tattoos, so she can say anything and they'll still think it's sexy.

—I don't like that.

—Why?

—Because it's weird.

—I can teach you something else.

—Can you teach me how to say I want to hit you with a block of tofu?

She thinks about it while chewing.

—买一块豆腐撞死你。

—买一块豆腐撞死你?

—Do you know what that means? It's an idiom for when someone is hopeless. Someone's situation is so hopeless you might as well just hit them with a block of tofu.

I want to hit you with a block of tofu, I say over and over until we pull up to our house just as the first drop of rain hits the ground.

In Chinese, the words for appetite and desire share the same characters. 欲望. I don't know what this means, but I want to believe that everything I long for, I long for using my mouth.

Before I met Jessica, I thought I wanted to become a Buddhist. Its main teaching is about karmic retribution, which means that every bad astral event is the aftermath of a lingering desire, and the only way to fully transcend suffering is to let go. But what happens if you do the opposite of what's instructed and allow yourself to be leashed to your longings? There are days where I can still feel my muscles straining to blossom under my skin. Someone told me a story once about a dog in Japan named Saihu who died while demonstrating to her owner that the duck he was about to consume was poisonous. She did this by snatching it out of his plate and consuming it herself.

You can see here that there is no clear border between desire and sacrifice. Nobody knows whether Saihu was trying to protect her owner or if she was just hungry, or if she were a savior or the canary in a coal mine. They sell duck at the butcher shop across the street from our apartment, and when Jessica is lazy, she buys one and eats it cold. I look outside and see the row of ducks lined up in the butcher's display, and I focus my gaze on the empty hook. She soaks each piece in black vinegar and spits the bones straight in the trash, mouthing her happiness out loud to me.

My mother used to tell me that if you bite your tongue on accident, it's your body telling you it wants to eat meat. A decade ago, when I first became a vegetarian, she would smack her lips and demand I show her my tongue, scolding me when she saw it was studded with blisters.

From a young age, I wanted to demonstrate my allegiance to animals; and as I grew older, I wanted to become completely ascetic, to eliminate all desires. There are so many desires to be maimed—the desire to kill, the desire to consume, the desire to mimic, the desire to forget, etc. The first time Jessica kisses me, it feels like all the blisters on my tongue are on fire. We woke up late in the afternoon, with the sun rippled on the sheets, and I lay there, in my paleness, shivering under the ceiling fan with her body hovering above mine.

Are you cold? she asked before jamming her shoe into the ceiling fan and bending down to bury her tongue back inside me.

———————————

On the freeway the rain makes the ground look blurry. The yellow lines pass clean through us, and Jessica keeps swerving when we come too close to the median. She's smoking a cigarette with the windows down so all the rain flies into her Pepto-Dismal truck. It hits her in the face with a special kind of fury. She looks tired from all the labor she's performing, and I want to help her, but I don't know how to drive stick and I don't really like to smoke.

—How long will it take?

—Thirty minutes, maybe more. Did you bring a book?

—I forgot.

She ashes out the window.

—I'll be even faster then.

We drive to the outskirts of East L.A. with the stereo in between two channels so the voices on the airwaves melt into each other. I can tell she knows the way from memory, so I lean my seat back and look at the sky. She usually does this at the end of every month alone, but I insisted on coming with her this time. So you can take the carpool lane, I said, but we both know that's not why I wanted to come.

When I open my eyes again we're parked in front of a one-story yellow house with a chain-link fence. She takes the key out of the ignition and turns to me.

—Hey. Thanks for coming. It's nice to not do this on my own.

—Of course.

I reach over and put my hand over hers on the gear stick. She holds it up and kisses my palm.

—I'll be back soon.

A long time passes, and I get anxious that something has gone wrong. I close my eyes and try to doze off, but instead I daydream about the taste of Jessica's mouth. When I kissed her for the first time last night, it tasted like a carnal loneliness. Keywords: slaughter, morning dew. I think about the way Jessica slices fruit, how she never uses a cutting board, just holds the dripping wet peach in her hand and plunges the knife in, gouging out the pit and sucking the juice out first. I've never met someone who eats fruit with such casual excess, like an animal living between the meat world and the real world.

Just as I've resolved to get out and go look for her, Jessica comes running out of the house shrieking and laughing. When the car door opens she throws all the cash into my lap. She puts the key in the ignition and I look at the dashboard and realize it hasn't even been twenty minutes yet.

—Look how rich we are, baby.

Her cheeks are sweaty and tinged with red.

—That's it? You're finished?

—He was quick this time because his wife got off work early.

She laughs some more and starts the engine.

Just when we're pulling away, a man comes out of the

yellow house and waves at us with his belt half-unbuckled. I think it's Mr. Calcagni, but I can't see past the rain. He's wearing camouflage pants and his belly juts out of his tight polo shirt. Our rent is due tomorrow and we had to choose between pawning her mother's jewelry or having groceries next week. No we don't, Jessica said, and winked at me before picking up the phone.

Jessica rolls her window down to smoke. The money flutters in my lap like lilies in a shallow lagoon. She can't stop laughing, while doing a cartoon imitation of him picking up his wife's call and rushing her out the door with his clothes barely on. I laugh with her, but secretly I want to say a quiet prayer for all the Mr. Calcagnis of the world, buckling their belts just in time to say goodbye.

———————————

Lately I have dreams of rooms that are empty. In these rooms, bodies are printed in traces but nobody is there. Bed linens, a book that's been used as an ashtray, an ashtray that's been used as a coin holder, a coin holder with nothing except pennies, etc. I like the hollowed-out emptiness of a room that's been tinged with use.

But I want to have dreams of beds that are full. When I first moved into Jessica's, I accidentally shattered a mirror in my bed when I was trying to hang it on the wall. I was so depressed back then I just fell asleep, with incredible stillness, curled around the shards. In my sleep I stirred with the same subconscious care I practice when I'm lucky enough to have someone else asleep beside me.

Sometimes I have dreams of flowers growing in the desert. I want Jessica to drown them in water until they grow as thick as jungles.

———————————

Walking home from CVS that evening, I look up and witness the sky for the first time all week. There isn't anything pouring out of it tonight. The electric blue stains the clouds, and I see the hazy outline of a sun slipping into the earth. The sidewalk is full of worms and cicadas that have emerged from the long grass to drink the rain. I walk slowly, with my eyes pressed to the sidewalk, trying not to crush anything with a soul.

A block from home, I leap across a puddle and see two enormous frogs splashing inside of it. Their dimpled skin and yellow eyes gaze back at me, as if they recognize me from a past life. The frogs have a pattern of black speckles lining their backs like watermelon seeds, and I think they must be siblings, or maybe lovers, because sometimes you've been with someone for so long you can begin to morph into the same being.

I put my bag down and crouch to their level, studying the architecture of their skins. They are slightly iridescent, glazed over in a layer of oil.

—Are you lost?

I look around and there is no swamp in sight. I could have mistaken their patch of water for a mirage lake. Before they have a chance to answer, a truck comes speeding past, splashing water all over the three of us. I open my mouth to scream.

— Do you want to get us killed?

The frogs croak absently. Someone else flips me off for blocking the road.

—Hold on, let me take you somewhere safe.

My fingers are hot and alien, but the frogs don't resist my touch. Their bodies barely fit in my palms, so I cradle them wetly in my sweatshirt as I run back to the house. As soon as I kick open the front door, I rush to the bathtub and run a thin layer of cool water, only deep enough to submerge them. I plop them down gently and watch the water ripple.

—Do you like the temperature? I can make it warmer or cooler.

—

—Good. I like this temperature, too.

I sit cross-legged beside the tub and peer over the edge, squinting at their bodies under the dim yellow light. I notice a long scar on one frog's back, the cut deepening over his shoulder blade.

—That scar looks pretty rough. Did it hurt?

The frogs hop idly.

—You must not feel pain the same way I do.

—

—Did you get that cut from a lawnmower? You're lucky you still have your limbs.

I can see their necks pulsing with air, expanding in tune with their heartbeats. I wonder if they know they aren't in the puddle anymore, if they recognize the feeling of being transported elsewhere.

—I know a girl with a scar like that, too. It's on her forehead. She got it when she fell into the deep end of a swimming pool.

I splash some water over them to moisten their skins.

—Don't worry, she survived. Her mom looked out the window at just the right moment and ran out and dived in.

I trace my fingers along the surface and watch how the water bends under my weight. The frog with the scar blinks at me. He looks angry in the pale light of the bathroom. I imagine Jessica's mother pulling her out of the pool, her bright blood leaking onto the concrete, and nothing else.

Outside, the pork buns have been left out all week and are beginning to rot. I can smell their stench emanating from the living room altar—the scent of curdled meat fills the air, sour and heavy. In that moment, I can't believe how hungry I am. I rise slowly from the bathroom floor, knowing I am just empty enough for them to enter me.

SALLY BROWN, MAGOFFIN COUNTY, KENTUCKY.
PHOTOGRAPH BY GLORIA BAKER FEINSTEIN.

Thresholds

CARYN MIRRIAM-GOLDBERG

My friend stumbles from bed to table to bed,
his sister-in-law again explaining to him
why he can't go up the stairs anymore
or down the summer street without clothes,
which don't make sense to him since crossing
the threshold of all this pain.

A spray of lightning bugs ignites broken stitches
across the dark, while I walk the gravel drive
to my mother-in-law's house to tell her aide
about her bouquet of mini strokes or something else
no one diagnoses because what would it matter now?

When I step over the threshold into my friend's house,
he puts his hand over his heart and bows.
He knows he's dying, and in a week or a month,
he'll be just an outline no one can fill between bed and table,
like my mother-in-law lingering for what will be
years until she also breathes her early morning over.

Outside all of this—inside, too—the gears of blossom
keep turning, all the doors continually open wide,
and not just to death or disappearance. The world
keeps telling us how much there is to step through.

Ode on an Urn

JOHN MOESSNER

When old age shall this generation waste,
  Thou shalt remain, in midst of other woe
  —John Keats

Rounded, like a bent knee, and smooth
like the matte feel of a room lit through
opaque glass. The geometry of something
shaped by hands, its curves always return
to itself. A body for a body, or a collection

of the body's elements: fire, sand, bone, earth.
Time is still underneath its closed lid, a fixed point,
a dark cavity, quiet, except for the dull
echo of the world outside, turning, turning
always forward toward some bright, fiery end.

Our Distinguished Judge
The *New Letters* Publication Award in Fiction

 Anthony Grooms has twice been the recipient of the Lillian Smith Prize for Fiction, and has been awarded a Sokolov Scholarship of the Bread Loaf Writers' Conference, the Lamar Lectureship of Wesleyan College, and an Arts Administration Fellowship by the National Endowment for the Arts. He is the author of the novels *The Vain Conversation* (Story River Books, 2018), *Trouble No More: Stories* (Octopoda/WOC Press, 2016), *Bombingham* (One World, 2002), and the poetry collection *Ice Poems* (Poetry Atlanta Press, 1988). He teaches creative writing and literature at Kennesaw State University in Atlanta, Georgia. We are grateful for his service in judging the submissions to the *New Letters* Publication Award in Fiction.

Primates

D O N N A   G O R D O N

It's the opening day of the new rain forest exhibit at the Franklin Park Zoo in Boston, and Nikki, the thirteen-year-old daughter of my fiance, Brian, leans as far as she can against the Plexiglas wall, exhaling cold air in circular bursts. The gorilla in the simulated rain forest has warm brown eyes the color of melted chocolate. Green ferns jut around her face, framing it like a spiky flower. Her eyes shift thoughtfully from side to side.

Nikki stares, with the empathy of a child, as if trying to absorb the gorilla's gestures into her face. Finally, Nikki draws back and lets her head sink into her shoulders. "I wish I knew what she was trying to say." Nikki turns to me, eyebrows knitted together.

Brian and I are spending the weekend with Nikki because her mother, Audrey, an expert on Cinquecento painting, was unexpectedly called to Florence to help authenticate some fragments of drawings suspected to have been done by Raphael. There is speculation, however, principally visible in the treatment of the hands, that they were not by him after all, but by a teenage boy, an apprentice to another master draughtsman.

Nikki is thirteen going on twenty-five. Blond and slim in her nymphet prime, she is filled with disdain for most things, especially adults and food. In the Bird House amid the tuxedoed penguins and orange-beaked toucans, she complained about the smell of naphthalene. Outside, the water at the fountain is too warm. She is watching her weight, and will only eat soup and salad and popcorn.

Moisture is forming inside the big glass picture window that seals the gorilla's man-made atmosphere, complete with artificial sky and sun. The whole rain forest environment is controlled by a series of machines that function like heart and lungs. The blue slate wall outside is already scribbled with caveman graffiti: *hubba hubba, ugh,* and *Tarzan was here.* In the distance I see Brian, who has gone to get hot chocolate for all of us, standing beneath a red-and-white striped awning, balancing three white Styrofoam cups in his right hand, while a small, bearded man with fingerless gloves counts out change.

By profession Brian is a commodities trader, a member of that breed of legalized gamblers who risk fortunes every day. He has remarkably good legs for a man. Brian is a purist. He doesn't trade pork bellies or orange juice or grains. He trades for himself: gold and silver, the euro, Deutsche mark, yen, Swiss franc.

The thirst for danger runs in his family. Three months ago in September, when Brian first hired me through a referral from my friend Margo to help decorate his new house in Lincoln, and we were just beginning to get to know each another, he told me this incredible story. How in 1609, his Dutch ancestor on the boat to America overheard the captain say that whoever touched land first would be king—so he chopped off his hand with an axe and threw it to shore. This is the stock that Brian is made of.

Now Nikki turns toward the gorilla and squishes up her face in an ape-like way. The dark beast stares back with a leaden, depressed gaze. Her brown eyes roll slightly, moist and oily as olives.

Nikki leans still farther over the railing, making the signs of the deaf language with her fingers, thumb and forefinger contorted into oval and triangular shapes, gestures she learned in her seventh-grade class for *peace and love*. It strikes me then that the way people behave with animals is the way they secretly want to be treated themselves—with utter calm and indulgence.

"I think we need the Universal Translator," I say to Nikki. "You know, like on *Star Trek*." Referring, of course, to the original series still playing in reruns—not the hackneyed version that came afterward, in which everyone's alien makeup is so transparent you can see where their ordinary human features begin behind the ears.

"That's right," Nikki says, looking past me into the creature's beleaguered face. "Spock was able to speak to sheer energy, invisible blobs. He could figure out alphabets he never heard of."

The gorilla's steel-gray fur is matted and glistening. Fine gray hairs form a beard under her chin. She stares out with an unmistakably human look of doom.

"We really come from Africa," Nikki glares defiantly, pushing a wisp of stray blond hair off her forehead, arching fists against the rail. "Leakey knew that. We're all black at heart."

"You might be right," I say. "Darwin might agree." At thirteen, she is almost my height. If we were a few years closer in age we might be sisters, heroines side by side with long flowing hair and O-mouthed expressions of surprise in a novel by one of the Brontës. We are in many ways physically alike. Though I am twelve years older, and though we are not identical feature for feature, one might suspect by the look in our faces that we are thinking along the same lines.

Finally, just when Nikki appears to have given up making contact with the gorilla, the animal miraculously responds by intertwining her fingers. It seems finally she understands. *The gorilla's words are in her eyes.*

"Look," Nikki shrieks, as the animal gestures to her. "She's trying to tell me something."

Now Brian sneaks up behind both of us. "How are my girls?" he says, and we both turn around to face him. Ordinarily, they see one another on Sunday afternoons and Tuesday nights. It seems they share a private code.

When Brian and Audrey got divorced nine years ago, he gave her everything—the house, the jewels, the Civil War relics, including the old musket and gun from the battle of Lexington and Concord. According to Brian, Audrey was a social climber who wanted him to scale the corporate ladder with suction cups. He wanted to go out on his own, which meant taking big chances with the markets, risking the possibility he might lose everything.

After Brian moved out, he was broke for a year and lived in a rooming house in Brighton. Audrey used to bring Nikki to him on Sundays. Nikki was only four and would stand shyly in the doorway looking up at the ceiling, completely unaware of the depth of his decline. "Don't worry Daddy, it's all right," she'd said. "Things will be all right again." That still gets to him, even now.

Later that year, in April, when Brian went short on gold, he made such an obscenely large fortune that if he were smug and artless he'd consider himself set for life.

After the divorce, Nikki was the only real woman in his life. She watched the girlfriends come and go in waves of Prada and Chanel. As she got older, she counted on the fact that her father's girlfriends, while beautiful, didn't have the stamina to keep up. They lasted a year at most. But now after only six months, Brian and I have become engaged, and I think this has proven to be tremendously disappointing to her.

I had gotten the referral from my friend Margot, for whose design firm I'd interned after dropping out of the School of the Museum of Fine Arts, where I'd studied painting for two years, but could no longer justify the cost of tuition. I had student loans, a car payment, and a room in a rooming house overrun by mice. Before going to work for Margot, the only kind of decorating I had done was with colored frosting on a birthday cake. But I soon learned the difference between chintz and toile, and after three years on her payroll was starting to earn a decent paycheck, though the idea of indulging the whims of the rich was foreign and somewhat abhorrent. I had covered the walls of my own apartment in the Back Bay with life-sized posters of the "Venus de Milo" and slept with a mattress on the floor. It was the first winter I'd indulged and bought a new winter coat and snow boots.

Margot, ten years older and far more experienced, was an old friend of Brian's family, and was in over her head with a slew of unfinished McMansions dotting the Northeast corridor. Mostly I worked on small-scale apartments for single men or women on Beacon Hill or in the South End, living on a budget. It wasn't until much later I realized she'd set us up.

That day I pulled up in front of the house on Sandy Pond Road. It was late September. I could see when I turned up the circular drive and saw the magnolias past bloom, and the pond stretched out in the distance, that the house was much too big for a single man. It struck me as art in the abstract, the way a house appears staged in a movie.

I sat there in my Honda Civic with the motor running, not wanting to get out. Then the lights came on, illuminating the foyer windows, and Brian opened the door. He was tall and good looking, the way Wasps who live perfect expensive lives and never run out of money are portrayed in Tourneau watch ads in *The Times*.

I was recovering from a bad case of laryngitis, and even though I had forewarned Brian about this over the phone and tried to reschedule, he had insisted on keeping the appointment. My voice was strained and raw as we went from room to room and I took inventory on my iPad. He brushed against my shoulder accidentally, trying to get a closer look at a wallpaper catalog open in my hands. Clues are everywhere—in a person's choice of clothes, in the color of their eyes, in their pets. Some clients are willing to take a risk, while others just want matching everything from front door to backyard.

After briefly surveying the grounds, we went back inside and sat opposite one another on the bare oak floor in the empty living room, our legs folded beneath us, as the last of the afternoon light disappeared behind the wall of glass framing the hills. Pretty soon Brian stopped talking, stopped concentrating, as we leafed through sample books of wallpaper and paint. All the time he had had this strange involuntary grin spreading wider across his face that he seemed helpless to control, as if none of this mattered, as if he were seeing something else.

"I think I may have known you in another life," he said finally, searching my face. "Do you believe in that sort of thing?"

"Not really," I said, thinking it was a line.

But two weeks later, by the time the parchment-colored Roman shades were on order along with the Iranian tabriz, we were lovers.

At first Brian and I thought we'd fill the house with furniture and give it that overstuffed look that's pictured in *New England Home.* But night after night, watching the empty rooms slowly fill up with violet, golden light reflected off the water, the more it became obvious that the pond itself was an inhabitant.

The truth is, Brian and I come from dramatically different backgrounds. My mother was a small-town housewife, my father a used car salesman. I had to work after school as a clerk in a sporting goods shop to help my mother pay the bills after he died. Choosing art school instead of college was completely impractical. Though I loved to draw, there was no way I could trade a good likeness of someone's face or hands for a reliable paycheck.

Brian is Wasp to the core—his bone marrow is probably laced with ivy. Harvard College and Harvard Business School. His father had a seat on the New York Stock Exchange and was briefly a candidate for governor.

Brian didn't tell me about Nikki right away. It was early morning, the light just starting to fill out the corners of the room. I went downstairs and found a note next to the coffee pot: "Be back soon with a special breakfast treat." An hour later, he showed up with Nikki. I was only wearing a robe and felt naked and humiliated.

I wanted to kill him then and there for having kept her a secret. What kind of man would do that? What kind of father? What kind of fiancé, for that matter?

As she stood there in the hallway looking small and dark, and casting an uncertain shadow, I began to understand that he hadn't told her about me either.

"Nice to meet you, Nikki," I said, stunned by the reality of her flesh and blood. "Your father's told me so much about you. I'm glad to meet you finally."

Brian stood leaning against the newly painted ecru wall, looking only slightly guilty. The house had a ghostly feel that time of day, with gray light reflected off the lake—already frozen solid though it was only mid-December.

"I stopped first and got bagels. Want to go for a skate before breakfast?"

Nikki and I just looked at each other. She had come into the light, and I could see she was tall and lean, her eyes pale green, her long blond hair loosely twisted into a braid. She was wearing a scoop-neck shirt that hugged her thin body like a leotard.

"You know I don't eat carbs," she said, directing her eyes toward my stomach. "The last thing I would want is to look like a middle-aged fraulein."

"Nikki," Brian warned. "Play nice. If anything, you and Jess look like sisters."

He was right.

"Dad's always doing stuff like this," Nikki said, coolly, asserting her long-term knowledge of him. "You're not the first. He's had a thousand girlfriends, you know."

"Nikki!" Brian said. "Enough! You two don't mind, do you, if I go take a quick spin across the ice?"

She looked around at the nearly empty living room. "Dad said you've ordered furniture and stuff. I like it better like this. In my mom's house everything's an antique. My mom likes quilts and old things. She says I'm like her divining rod. She points me in the direction at flea markets and antique shows and I find her something good."

"Maybe you can help me with this place," I said. "We'll make it cosier."

"Sure," she said, looking down at her shoes. "But this house is too big for just Dad, don't you think? No offense, but I don't know how long you'll be around."

The late afternoon sky was darkening with amber and violet streaks. Together we moved to the window, where a handful of bare, white birches stood out like a circle of white candles around the jagged ellipse of the pond. We could barely spot Brian edging out onto its mirrored surface. We stood there saying nothing for a few long awkward minutes, somehow frozen but separate, until the sun was completely out of sight.

Later that night, after Brian returned Nikki to her mother's house in Cambridge and Audrey's distinguished new husband, Mylo—a third-generation Cantabridgian with a salt-and-pepper beard and a trust fund—I confronted him.

"How could you not tell me?" I demanded. "What other secrets are you keeping from me?"

I poured myself a glass of wine and sat on the floor in front of the fire in the empty living room. Some of the new furniture was due to arrive later that week—an extra-long burgundy velvet sofa, two club chairs and a rug imported from India woven entirely from deconstructed saris. There were only the brass beds upstairs, the pots and pans in the kitchen, a set of pewter candlesticks.

Brian put down his scotch on the mantle and used tongs to add a log to the fire. I got the feeling that this was all a joke to him, no more than a puzzle to be solved, like playing the markets. Isn't that what gamblers are good at, playing hide and seek with the truth?

"I should have told you, Jess," Brian said, coming to sit across from me on the floor, "right from the get-go. But I was scared you'd run and I didn't want to risk it. I know it looks bad, but I didn't exactly know how to tell you. Then I figured everything would get sorted out if I just brought her here."

"And have us stand around like idiots?"

"It wasn't my intent. I love you both. Lots of people have blended families these days. C'mon, you can handle it."

"Maybe," I said. "Maybe not. That's not the only problem. Haven't you noticed how much we look alike? Or are you the kind of father who wants to sleep with his daughter? You've got two of us, an extra, like a baker's dozen or something. And what about Audrey? I haven't met her yet. Are we three versions of the same face?"

He moved closer to try to kiss me, but I put up my hand.

"I wanted to surprise you later, but now I can see I shouldn't wait," he said. "We're going to NYC next weekend. I bought us tickets to the new exhibit of Raphael's drawings opening at the Met."

He strode to his bookcase and pulled out a tome of Raphael's drawings, the book I'd savored since high school and had brought here from my apartment.

"I know how much you love his work, and when I heard about the exhibit in New York, I had to get you in to see it."

I moved closer to the window, feeling the force of freezing temperatures pressed against the glass. The criss-crossed shape of my arms cast a shadow in the shape of an "x" that traveled the length of the living room floor.

It occurred to me that he was doing with me what he would do with Nikki if she were there: divert from the situation and then try and buy her off. How long had it been since I had been to New York and seen anything? Or spent a night in a hotel and walked down 5th Avenue? These were all unattainable before I met Brian. Despite my reservations, I loved that he knew me and what would make me happy.

"And with Nikki being such a big part of your life, how do you manage to keep things civil with Audrey?" I asked.

"Look, it's all very easy," he said. "We split Christmas and Thanksgiving and every other weekend. Nikki likes being with Mylo's family. They're a bunch of artists and professors. They do things by the book and are boring and conventional."

"She doesn't even want to get to know me," I said. "Do you see the way she glares? I'm not interested in being someone's wicked stepmother."

"Please don't be angry or hurt," Brian said. "Can we give it some time?"

I could bail, I thought. I could run now and avoid a host of other problems. It wasn't his money that mattered, it hardly really registered. It was the feeling I'd had since the day I met him that I was no longer adrift, that I belonged with someone finally, that when he looked at me something cut clear to the bone.

Sometimes, on the weekend, when Brian and I pick up Nikki in front of her mother's understated Cambridge Victorian, she is already waiting on the wooden porch in a wild oversized outfit. Then sometimes she refuses to come out at all, and Brian has to go to the door and persuade her, and she'll put old sweat pants over her pajamas and tie her head with a scarf and sit blindfold in the back of the car making animal noises. Then Brian will grunt and sputter and ignore me until they both start laughing. He is her hero.

The problem is this: after weeks of staring at one another over tables at restaurants and at movies and zoos, it still feels impossible to break the ice. These efforts at friendship are exhausting. Perhaps I try too hard. She is a diplomat and will recite exciting stories of visitors who have come to her private progressive school that day and have taught her 7th-grade class how to throw clay pots or weave rugs or imitate sounds in nature like a Native American.

So far in our efforts to get to know one another, the three of us have been to two Japanese restaurants, one Chinese, and an old European Hungarian bistro for which Nikki was far too young but we smuggled her in anyway. We've been to more than one movie, starring unspeakably good-looking actors disguised as blood-sucking vampires and Nazi spies, portrayed by Tom Cruise, Brad Pitt, Justin Timberlake, the Bieber.

We've gone on a shopping spree at Bloomingdale's where Nikki and I both had makeovers at the Lancome counter and saw our newly sophisticated faces projected on a video screen, Brian examining the handiwork with pride.

"How many years apart are you two sisters?" the heavily made-up clerk asked, speculating between layers of purple eye shadow and black mascara.

Nikki's eyes clouded over and she made a fist with one hand.

"She is not my sister. She is a stereotype, a young woman who needs to hitch herself to an older man for security and fortune," she said, before bolting from the store.

The clerk shrugged. "I've seen it all," she said.

Brian looked at me with a combination of irritation and amusement. I had the feeling again that he enjoyed this rivalry.

Today the zoo is neutral territory. Being Saturday, it's filled with families on parade. You can pick out the single fathers by their frightened eyes and the way they hold their children's hands much too tight. The babies in their crochet pastel jumpsuits ride by in strollers like kings. I can't help but think that these infants somehow know more than we do, that they're somehow in rhythm with the beasts, that they still feed on the same knowledge.

Audrey's mother went to Smith and then Harvard and now teaches at a small state arts college in Massachusetts. Famous painters run in the family, wealthy philanthropists, people who sit on the boards of major museums. I have never met Audrey, but from what I gather she is composed and dresses entirely in Ralph Lauren.

Soon the gorilla appears to have fallen asleep next to some fake-looking large gray rocks, the kind that Superman could demolish with his pinky. We exit the main path and walk slowly out the wrought-iron gate toward the parking lot, past the snorting gray elephants and pituitary giraffes, their soft triangular heads lost in the mossy tops of trees.

We drive west out Route 2 in the fading light, past the rust-colored elms and jaundiced oaks. In late fall, New England begins to ready itself for loss. Already I have moved some of my things into the master bedroom, and I sense that Nikki is not happy about this. She is silent for the first fifteen minutes of highway, slumped in the middle of the back seat as though she is saying to me *I hate you* between her teeth. She opens *The Times* to the travel section, checking the temperature in Florence, going down the column past Brussels and Delhi to see that it is a brusque 55.

"I hope my mother doesn't get abducted by terrorists," she says, shuddering. "Those little Italian men are always driving around in black cars and snatching people off the streets, holding them ransom. I was there once. In Florence, I mean," and her eyes grow animated. "My mother was finishing her research, and we walked all over the city and had *gelato* twice a day. I've already seen Michelangelo's

'David,'" she confides in a whisper, "the real one, not the copy outside in the plaza near the Uffizi. I touched the David's foot once when the guard wasn't looking. It was bigger than my whole arm."

By now we've pulled up in front of the large yellow colonial manned by two-foot-wide columns and a circular drive. The house itself is a force beyond reason—with its palatial foyer, sunken living room, formal dining room, eight bedrooms, and four baths. Not to mention a maid's kitchen and separate carriage house.

Brian unloads the car, pops the rear, and I see that Nikki has packed a black overnight bag the size of Houdini's trunk. She gives me a scathing look and hauls it upstairs to her room and locks herself in. A huge room with twin brass beds and absolutely nothing on the walls. By comparison, her tiny attic room at home hosts her various collectibles: antique hats, her great-grandmother's old, high-button shoes, a dress mannequin with the near-expressionless face of a colonial rag doll.

It's Saturday night and Nikki is sleeping over for the next few nights, and I'm making my special mystery pizza from scratch. My hands are pasty, and I am covered with flour up to my elbows, as I knead the dough and it bounces back. Brian has built a fire in the living room, while Nikki sits at the kitchen table studying seventh-grade math problems with dogged intensity, as if she truly believes the world is made up of these invisible shapes and balanced equations. Brian is good with math.

I remove the pizza from the oven—its intoxicating smells of garlic and oregano scent the air—and set it on the table. Nikki refuses to try it. "No thanks," she says, faking sweetness—and helps herself to a stick of celery from the platter of raw vegetables instead.

"Sure you don't want anything else, Sweetie?" Brian asks across the counter, gazing affectionately. She reaches to hug him, one arm stretched long and gorilla-like around his neck. "No thanks, Daddy," she says. "We have dance tryouts this week at school and you know how it is, a leotard shows everything. I don't want to show up wearing a slice of pizza or a hot dog or hamburger."

I look at Brian with lingering doubt, wondering why he's not on her case to eat, wondering if he even knows what anorexia is. And what about Audrey?

Later that night we sit in the pitch-dark living room watching *Rear Window* on cable, while countless white stars illuminate the blackened sky over the lake. It's almost like living with a third person. The water changes constantly and has distinct moods. Brian sits in the middle of the sofa, and Nikki and I sit on either side. Part of my desire to win Nikki over has to do with my depth of feeling for Brian—despite the omission. Since I met him my emotions are no longer my own. I am afraid I will never feel that way again, complete in my bones, shattered in a spectacular way.

During the scary part of the movie, where the murderer Raymond Burr is coming up the stairs to kill Jimmy Stewart, who is trapped in a wheelchair, I am surprised at how fragile Nikki is, how her eyes flash with fear. As the tension heightens, she covers her eyes with her hands.

"I can't look," she yells.

"It's OK, " I say. "In a few minutes it will all be over."

I look over at Brian who winks back, as if to say he's got it all under control. I smile uneasily, weighed down by the undercurrent of what I still haven't been able to explain. How as long as Nikki puts herself between us, the more I feel divided against myself, surprised by the degree of understanding I feel for her, despite her bad behavior. After my father died, my mother shocked me by insisting on her right to fall in love again, and joined a group called Parents Without Partners. Soon our lives were littered with the Fred Flintstones and Mr. Magoos of the unnatural world. I will never forget the sense of theft I felt, watching my mother being stolen right out from under me, by men who didn't seem to have the right to be part of our lives, or know the slightest thing about her.

Later, after Nikki has silently gone up to bed, and Brian and I lie naked in the dark watching the ancient medallion of moon scrape the wooden beams of the ceiling, I whisper to him that though I am in love with him, I am afraid that Nikki and I will never be friends. She will never break.

"She's just a kid, " Brian said, arm stretched beneath the weight of my neck and shoulders. "All kids are ready to love, just be yourself; be patient a little longer."

"That's not it," I say. "She's dead set against me. You've lived a charmed life. You have no idea what it's like to watch your mother or father find another partner and go about life like it's business as usual. Even if Audrey already has Mylo. A kind of loneliness sets in. I can't explain."

The next morning, Sunday, when Nikki comes downstairs, Brian has already gone out for a run. I'm in the kitchen alone in jeans and a white T-shirt making blueberry pancakes and coffee. I want to tell her to eat something. I want to tell her that we are more alike than different. I want to tell her *I know.*

She stands in the doorway in black leggings and a long, oversized maroon sweatshirt that falls clumsily off one shoulder. The thin bones of her wrists protrude, and her pale eyes are drawn up dramatically at the edges with kohl black liner, as though she's trying on a role. She walks into the kitchen and suddenly stops. A deadness floods her gaze for a few long seconds. Then she raises her left hand above her head, and pirouettes toward me in a fleeting whirl, moving so quickly I'm afraid she won't stop.

"That looks pretty professional," I say, stepping aside at the last second, knowing this performance is rooted in defiance. "Thanks," she says, and wordlessly walks to the coffee pot, sniffs it for a second, then helps herself to a cup.

A little spills on the counter and she looks backward across her shoulder to see if I'm watching as she wipes it up with a sponge. If Audrey were here I'm sure that the coffee would be replaced by milk. Nikki sips it slowly at the kitchen counter. A few minutes later, when she hears Brian coming through the front door and depositing his keys on the hall table, she gets up and stashes it furtively in the sink.

"How's everyone doing?" he says, coming into the kitchen a little out of breath, cheeks scarred red from pushing against the wind. But he soon senses the all-too-familiar divide.

"Just waking up," I say, reaching to hand him a cup of coffee, giving him a kiss on the cheek. "Thinking about a plan," I add. "Seeing as we've got the whole day together."

"How about you, kiddo?" Brian asks Nikki. "Got any ideas?"

"Whatever you two want is fine," she says. "You two go ahead. I may stay in and do my homework."

Brian and I eat breakfast while Nikki keeps her nose in a book. Nothing moves. In the sunroom in the corner closest to the window, she sits on the sofa growing smaller and smaller, immersed in words. Dark clouds crowd the sky over the lake in gray shades the color of the Confederacy. By the time I've finished reading the paper and have had a second cup of coffee, the afternoon still looms in front of us, vacant and unavoidable.

For a while, after I had started wetting my feet in the design trade—but before I met Brian—I used to go on Sunday afternoons to the Venetian courtyard of the Isabella Stewart Gardner Museum along the Fenway and sketch the gardens. Deep blue-violet hydrangeas criss-crossed with silver Artemesia, and nearby red and yellow Guzmania—its vase-shaped rosettes engineered to store water. Marble and bronze statues of Persephone and Odysseus. Time gave way to feeling and I was accountable to no one. Now I look at the two of them and remembered that state of existence without judgment. If I mattered to someone else, did that mean I mattered to myself? Was mattering the same as being in love?

Despite the engagement ring, despite the sex, the house with the circular drive—all of it—the way he touches me now will never be the same. I look at Brian and see something different than what I saw before. I don't think it occurs to him.

"Why don't we take a walk around the lake," Brian suggests, pushing his chair back from the table where he's been studying the financial pages. "Something that will get us up and out of the house. Pretty soon these trees will be completely bare," he says, gesturing out the window with a note of sadness. "One more week and it'll all be over."

"Why not," I say. "I'm game for a walk. Nikki?"

"We can be like Thoreau," Brian continues, reaching for his coat. "He camped out on this exact same spot on Sandy Pond one hundred years ago before moving down the road to Walden. Maybe we'll discover something he left behind," he says trying to pique Nikki's curiosity. "Like a fossil or a skull."

Nikki shrugs and closes her book, leaving *Lord of the Flies* behind. Her eyes glaze over and her shoulders narrow, resembling for a moment yesterday's gorilla in the zoo, as she steps into her boots and puts on her parka.

We head out the back door across the shorn field dried to the color of hay, taking the path to the right single file. The trees are brown and skeletal, without a soul in sight. Brian is first to lead, picking his way carefully around the stone border of the lake. The ground is frozen beneath our feet, leaving only faint imprints, as though we are weightless, as though we are invisible. Above us, squirrels move in and out of trees, warning the others in the quiet that we are coming.

From time to time one of us stoops to show each other something marred by predators—the frail skeleton of a bat, calcified remains of a bird, leaf patterns imprinted in rock. Vines hang down in places that block our path and we brush them aside.

Nikki walks between us, but her heavy boots slow her down. After we have hiked nearly three-quarters of a mile around, the sky has begun to lose light, and Brian stoops to re-lace his boot. Nikki chooses this moment to run on ahead, declaring she wants to lead.

"Wait," he calls, "let's stay together . . . "

She has run off so fast that we have to hurry to keep up. Soon we've lost sight of her.

"Now what?" I say to Brian, who is worried but not worried.

"Nikki has walked this trail umpteen times," he says, his palms empty. "The whole thing is barely three miles around. She's not going to get lost, trust me."

"Are you sure?" I ask, surprised by my growing anger. "Did it ever occur to you how much she must hate us? Hate me? That maybe it's not cool to have your daughter see you've picked a girlfriend who's so much like her? And to have your girlfriend see how much she resembles your daughter? What message does that send? Do you think either of us feels loved?"

"Now wait a minute," he starts off. "You're overreacting. You don't need to be her mother and you don't need to be her friend. Can't you just try a little harder to make it work?"

"For who?" I say. "For you? You waited a month to tell me you were a father! You have no right to ask anything. But I still care enough about Nikki to go and look for her. She's probably so upset she's freezing somewhere."

"I know my daughter better than anyone," he says. "I'm sure she's OK somewhere, just pretending."

We walk together in silence toward the direction she has gone off in. After five minutes, it seems Nikki doesn't want to be found. "Let's split up," I say. "You go that way and I'll continue here. Let's synchronize watches and meet back in ten minutes."

I pick my way among the speckled roots, following the scent of running water, past tangled branches frozen solid in ice. When I can no longer see the top of Brian's red wool hat bobbing like a flare between us, I stop walking and stand still long enough to catch my breath, then look up to see a few new flakes of snow begin to falter. I feel light-headed—coming apart—as if I've traded something I couldn't understand for coming to know how I really feel.

I continue walking, stoop to test the earth beneath my boot where it springs back—damp, alive. When I look up again, I see a snarled cluster of branches directly ahead that appears to have been broken unnaturally by human hands.

I pry them apart, come upon a tunnel of narrow birches somehow dry, preserved, protected by a layer of evergreens feathered with snow. In the distance I can make out a human shape. It's Nikki crouched under a tangle of brush stripped clean of leaves. She turns, startled by the sound, and I see she's crying.

I move to put my arm around her shoulder tentatively, and am surprised at how thin it is. She flinches, turns toward me, her eyes wild.

"Look, Nikki," I say, seizing her by the shoulders. "There's something I want you to know. I'll never mean half as much to your father as you do. I'll never be as pretty, or as wise, or as talented. I'll never be . . . you . . . "

"But it's you he loves," she shouts. "He *chose* you. I know he did."

"Don't be so sure," I start to say, wishing I could reassure her. "I have to choose him back. I don't even know if that's what I want to happen. He's pretty mixed up as far as I can tell."

"Are you leaving, too . . . " she begins. But before I can answer, we're interrupted by the crash of breaking branches scraping the air behind us, as Brian staggers into the clearing, his head and shoulders weighted down by a layer of wet leaves the texture of fur.

"Finally," he says. "Finally, I found you two, I've been looking all over! And here you are having a tea party in the woods."

Nikki and I say nothing for a second, amazed at how clueless he is. Then we look at each other and burst out laughing.

"What's so funny?" Brian asks.

"Dad," Nikki says, "I'll give you a hint. It looks like you're wearing a wig. A bad one."

"Jeez," he says, pulling the stray leaves loose. "Thanks a lot. C'mon. It's getting late. If we're lucky, by the time we make it back to the house the ice will be perfect."

One thing the three of us have in common is we love to skate. The pond itself is a mystery. Once, Brian and I found pure white sand where you'd least expect it, buried under leaves, a circle of it, like a cove. Pure white sand soft as talcum.

It's near dusk when we kneel at the pond's frozen edge to pull on our skates. The sky is darkening overhead, violet and umber with a heart of steel, and Nikki and I have still not made peace.

We stand on the shore adjusting our laces, watching the waning gibbous moon begin its ascent, arcing steeply over the darkened hills. At the last minute, when the three of us are poised to begin to sweep across the ice, Brian stops short, holds up his bare hands.

"You two go ahead," he calls, looking back over his shoulder. "I forgot my gloves."

Nikki starts first, then I follow. We skate out onto the open ellipse of the pond, approaching one another from opposite ends. She looks at me for a second, awkwardly, then nods and moves ahead, one black leg skidding over the ice like a fragile heron, her face flushed, arms wide. I skate toward her, steadily placing one foot after the next, steadily moving toward her against the wind. When we are within inches of one another, I reach for her hand and she meets me halfway, positioning her arms like a leading man, and we move awkwardly together in a tiny circle.

Her dark wool cap has sunk low over her forehead, and her sharp green eyes blur and lose focus a little as we momentarily glide across the ice hand-in-hand. I don't know if she is crying or if the cold has stung her eyes. For a quick second, I look back toward shore where Brian is standing alone on the frozen lawn, watching.

New Letters

A Magazine of Writing & Art

$2,500 Conger Beasley Jr. Award for Nonfiction

$2,500 Patricia Cleary Miller Award for Poetry

$2,500 Robert Day Award for Fiction

Deadline: May 18, 2020: Enter online
at www.newletters.org via Submittable.

PLEASE INCLUDE WITH EACH SUBMISSION:

• One cover sheet stating the genre and title of the essay or story. For poetry, please list the titles of each poem. Your personal information should not appear anywhere on the manuscript.

• The name of the file you upload should be the name of your manuscript or the number of poems in your entry.

RULES & NOTES:

• Entries in fiction and essay are not to exceed 8,000 words. One poetry entry may contain up to six poems. Poems need not be related.
• Manuscripts may not be subsituted or revised once uploaded.
• Refunds will not be given for withdrawn manuscripts.
• Entries must be previously unpublished.
• Multiple entries are welcome with appropriate fees.
• First entry includes a one-year subscription to *New Letters*.
• Entries from outside the United States receive all contest privileges except the subscription.
• Current students and employees at the University of Missouri-Kansas City, and current volunteer members of the *New Letters* and BkMk Press staffs are not eligible.

Previous final judges include Philip Levine, Ellen Bass, Benjamin Percy, Joyce Carol Oates, Kathleen Norris, Mary Jo Salter, Kim Addonizio, Carolyn Forche, Cornelius Eady, and Margot Livesey.

New Letters Literary Awards, University of Missouri-Kansas City,
5101 Rockhill Road, Kansas City, MO 64110

Poetry in Peace and Action

By H.C. Palmer

Book Review:

Empires, by John Balaban,
Copper Canyon Press, 2019.

When I read "Empires," the title of this book, I think of past tense and collapses. Empires that came and went. So, even before I read his new collection, I speculated that this is what poet John Balaban is getting at. Indeed, these poems, tell the story of demise. To set the tone, I will jump to Balaban's last poem, "Back Then." He imagines that our empire—the American empire—has ended. Listen to a single bird in an American desert just north of the Rio Grande River's Big Bend in southwest Texas: "A canyon wren, perched in a willow, / plied the dawn with inquiring song." That wren is singing, "Is anybody here?"

What currency does Balaban own to make such a dire prediction? Try this: He grew up in a tough and violent multicultural neighborhood in Philadelphia, but Balaban attended Quaker meetings, picketed the Army's biological-warfare center at Ft. Dietrick, Maryland, and debated John Birchers. In 1963, he was in the crowd at the Lincoln Memorial in Washington, D.C., for Martin Luther King's "I Have a Dream" speech, where, says Balaban, King confirmed the poet's "sense of another, possible society."

He was a freshman at Penn State when King was murdered. While at Penn State, he won a Woodrow Wilson scholarship to Harvard graduate school where he was involved in an oral skirmish with Secretary of Defense Robert McNamara, who was standing on the roof of a bullet-proof car shouting at the "ignorance" of students there. The American War in Vietnam was ramping up. Balaban's two best high school buddies schemed to dodge the draft.

Balaban believed he could make a difference, as he says, "by going to Vietnam rather than protesting in the United States." He asked his draft board to be classified as a conscientious objector, provided he could serve in the war zone in a peaceful and humanitarian way. The board approved. He was 25 years old in 1968 when he joined International Volunteer Services, teaching English to Vietnamese school teachers in remote Mekong Delta villages. He was wounded by bomb shrapnel from a U.S. plane during the Tet offensive. After recovery, he managed the Committee of Responsibility to Save War-Injured Children, a program referring wounded and napalmed children to hospitals in the States for surgical care and recovery.

In 1971, he received a grant from the National Endowment for the Humanities to return for another year to Vietnam, where he recorded traditional oral folk poems on a portable tape recorder, then translated them into English. He recorded 35 singers, men and women and children. The youngest was a boy of 5; the oldest, a woman nearing 80.

Balaban has translated two books of poems from Vietnamese to English, *Ca Dao Vietnam: A Bilingual Anthology of Vietnamese Folk Poetry* (1980) and *Spring Essence: The Poetry of Hô Xuân Huong* (2000). He is also founder and curator of the Vietnamese Nôm Preservation Foundation, dedicated to the digitization of Vietnam's ancient script where he was working in 2013, when called to deliver a eulogy and write a poem for General Võ Nguyên Giáp's funeral and memorial service. Hundreds were there, near General Giap's home, to hear Balaban speak and commemorate a former enemy general.

I can't help but think of Ezra Pound's caution to W.S. Merwin, when Merwin was 18 or 19 years old and a student at Princeton: "At your age," Pound said to him, "you don't have anything to write about. You may think you have a subject, but you don't know what it is yet" (*Southwest Review* interview, 1983). This to say that John Balaban has had something to write about for a very long time. For instance, *New Letters* published his poem "After Our War" in its summer 1975 issue—a poem ending with the question, "After our war, how will love speak?" By then, Balaban was 32. That poem is book-ended in *Empires*, 44 years later, in the summer 2019 issue of *New Letters* with "Returning After Our War," a poem that is arguably the pivotal poem of this collection.

The first poem in *Empires*, "A Finger," serves notice that America is in trouble. A finger tip discovered in the rubble of the Twin Towers after 9/11 is identified. The finger's owner's mother plants a tree in a garden—in her daughter's memory—and we are forewarned in these last two lines, "Some look on it and feel restored. / Others, when the wind lifts its leaves, want to scream." There are more trees to come—in 17 of the 31 poems—and each tree is a marker through time, a presage.

In "After the Inauguration, 2013," the poet travels south in a train—a black man had just taken America's most important oath—and passes through Civil War battlegrounds where Confederates had lost the war for their dream of racist empire. Another poem, "Christmas Eve and Washington's Crossing," celebrates the beginning of the end of England's Western world empire.

"Poetry Reading by the Black Sea" gives us a long list of empires, including the U.S. Navy, and acacia trees that "fragrance our evenings," he writes, "as poplar fluff floats / over imperial rubble. 'Only poetry lasts.'"

Balaban also translates two poems of Benjamin Fondane, from the Romanian, who waits in captivity for the Nazis to take him to Auschwitz, where he will die. Fondane had been searching, "for that impossible peace we lost once in a great orchard / with the tree of life flowering at its heart."

Then to Vietnam and "Returning After Our War," where from the rooftop of the Majestic Hotel in Saigon (now Ho Chi Minh City), he describes the Saigon River and the city and the view almost 50 years later. Everything has changed. Graham Greene's apartment building has been replaced by a "garish complex of glass and metal." Even the venerable Rue Tu Do, my own favorite street in Saigon during our war in Vietnam, has been renamed Great Uprising. The Majestic is surrounded by tall buildings. The poem's speaker can no longer see beyond the far bank of the river. "Back in the / American days," he writes, "rockets were sometimes launched at the / city from the mangrove swamps across the way."

"Returning After Our War" is a five-part poem that sweeps north to Hanoi. Balaban discovers his old Saigon friends are gone, "Gone

like smoke. Like incense," he says. In Hanoi, the poet discovers
that Vietnam has adopted the enemy's music—crowds in the streets
singing American songs, and, strangely, Duke Ellington's "Take the
'A' Train." Ancient banyans surround a lake. People are dancing in
the streets. "Several million of them died in the war," he writes. "But
now the streets are packed with strolling families, and I am so / glad
for them." Tiny Vietnam, conquered many times by many invaders,
recoups and survives America's attacks, recovers and assimilates.

Balaban retreats (emotionally) now and then to poems of other
times and places, especially those of his beloved New Mexico and the
high desert country draining the southbound path of the Rio Grande.
Old poems that comfort. Old friends. He takes a breath, but keeps
the nib moving. In "Anna Akhmatova Spends the Night on Miami
Beach," the poet finds a Stanley Kunitz translation of Akhmatova
poems on a park bench in Miami Beach. The copy has a blurb on
the back that says Akhmatova had survived "a revolution and two
world wars." Most interesting, however, is the revision Balaban has
made at the end of this poem since it was first published in *Locusts
at the Edge of Summer* (Copper Canyon Press, 2003), where he
finished with a description of how Akhmatova wished to describe
"her night's excursion / amid the loud hilarities, the trivial hungers /
at the end of the American century." In *Empires*, he ends the poem
by saying she longed for someone, "to whom she could describe her
night's excursion / amid the loud hilarities, the consuming hungers, /
arriving toward the end of the American era."

In his penultimate poem, "Looking for the Lights," spots of light
seem to float in the air and vanish, and a man stops his pickup,
shuts off the ignition, then listens to the truck's ticking engine as a
Border Patrol agent stops behind his vehicle; blue-and-white strobe-
lights flash him nearly blind. The man is saved from arrest by
convincing the officer he's American. The officer says, "He had never
seen the lights himself but knew people who had."

Balaban suggests that those mysterious Marfa Lights in West
Texas, sighted for centuries by natives and Spanish explorers
(invaders) but without a documented source, are a metaphor for what
lasts—"the lights the local Indians took for star people visiting earth."

"Looking for some peace of mind / was like searching for a cricket in a field," he writes in "Back Then." The same man climbs a ridge as the evening sky darkens under a full moon, and "moonlight seemed to pour from his nostrils. / He made camp there, sleeping that night in a mess of dreams, troubled with bat squeaks, / with wild burros braying along the nearby creek." As you should expect by now, when the voices stop, "that blasted tree, high on the mesa rim / —that writhed at dusk like a man crucified— / was a tree again, rocking in the wind."

One night, perhaps not too far in the future, somewhere north of a polluted Rio Grande River and near the bombed-out village of Marfa, Texas, infantrymen or women from another, conquering country, say, will see the Marfa Lights and be surprised. "They must be remnants of America," one will say, "maybe fires built by survivors to warm themselves this desert winter night." Another will say, "Or, they could be aliens. Perhaps they've been here forever."

Empires informs us of an apocalypse of our own making—a personal version of the recurring story of hubris—like stories first painted or chiseled onto the faces of sandstone, which lead us to this moment, right now.

Women in Dangerous Waters

By Deborah Bacharach

Book Review:

> *Boats for Women*, by Sandra Yannone,
> Salmon Poetry, 2019.

The poems in Sandra Yannone's *Boats for Women* intertwine personal stories of a woman who desires women and historical touchstones, most significantly the sinking of the *Titanic*. I also hear echoes of the literature of the queer canon, from *The Well of Loneliness*, *Bastard Out of Carolina*, and *Stone Butch Blues*. Well researched and full of intimate historical detail, Yannone's poems take on the complexities of what was (and often still is) forbidden love.

In the sestina "The Boy with the Top," Yannone shifts the meanings of the end words. On board the *Titanic*, she says, "the boy's pull string snakes / to the camera." Then Yannone moves us to political commentary with the "snakes of industry" and, seamlessly, to figurative language when the speaker, making love to another woman, says, "my tongue will snake / her skin."

"Lifeboat #9" draws on *Titanic* allusions with stanzas shaped like lifeboats deployed across the sea of the page, but the subject matter is gay sex:

> I don't know why
> all aren't seen
> as stunningly

> stunning
> in any human
> combination

> between lust
> & inconvenience
> between imperfect

    & oddly potent
    between stranger
    and merely strange

The enjambed line breaks propel the reader forward. Each little stanza bobs along on the page but is held together by the story that is being told, the escape.

    The title poem "Boats for Women," a prose poem, becomes incantatory, starting almost every line with "Yes" or "Sometimes" as Yannone addresses one of the main themes of the book: "Sometimes when I kiss her, I am leaving a yes on her lips to remind her that I will go down with the ship. Sometimes when she whispers yes, she is staying on board." The lovers struggle in a world that shuns and disparages their love. This leads to another theme, anger, as in the villanelle "Other Women," where the hard-hitting syllables of one of the repeating lines—"all day she splits into the hard to find"—keep the focus on the hard work of living in the unkind world.

    In "Providence, April 14, 1998," the speaker calls her mother on the anniversary of the speaker's wedding, which is also the anniversary of the *Titanic* hitting the iceberg. The iceberg the speaker is trying to avoid: "the Providence of last / summer's love now ringing in my ears / and all that week before spent convincing my mother that she [the lover] was just a friend." As the speaker hides from her family, she calls herself and the lover "survivors" of these dangerous waters.

    These poems do not paint a simplistic us/them view of being a sexual minority in an oppressive society. With the pressure of living a secret life, it is often the lover who is guilty of emotional betrayals. In "Thin Objects," Yannone writes:

    of the first woman
    who asked
    to kiss you,

    who whispered
    into the first minutes
    of the new day,

"We can't ever
talk about
this again,"

There are plenty of poems here about the wonders and joys of
knowing and loving yourself. "Sonnet Before and After Everything
Collides" ends with, "I square my shoulders to the frosted questions, /
the pulse of your name, your body's nocturnal shine." It feels like a
triumph to read the fun, playful, relaxed tone of "The Ablative Case,"
where the speaker announces, "I'm thinking about pink now because
I'm a natty butch girl / all grown up / because I wear neckties but
sometimes contemplate bows, because I like women. . . . "

One of my favorite comments about love between women comes
in a poem called "Halifax, 1917, Then and Never Again," which takes
as its main subject a fire that burns the town down, but the first
stanza is a triumph against such "man-made" disasters:

When I contemplate her face as producing
that smile, that outward manifestation of her breath,
I travel inside my own complicated anatomy, induce
what I can to give back to this love-scorched earth.

AT WISE BLOOD BOOKSELLERS, KANSAS CITY, MO., JAN. 10, 2020, PANEL
ABOUT KANSAS CITY'S LITERARY TRADITION: (L TO R) ROBERT STEWART,
ANGELA ELAM, WHITNEY TERRELL, KEVIN KOTUR.

A Low-Water Bridge in High Water

By Denise Low

Book Review:

On the Chicopee Spur: Poems, by Al Ortolani,
New York Quarterly Books, 2019.

*How Wally Lost His Thumb and the Boy Scouts
Became Cannibals: New and Selected Poems*,
by Al Ortolani, Spartan Press, 2019.

Al Ortolani is an accomplished poet with eight books over 40 years, including the two listed here, added recently to his opus: *On the Chicopee Spur* and *How Wally Lost His Thumb and the Boy Scouts Became Cannibals: New and Selected Poems*. Both titles show this poet's ability to engage readers and suggest his own charisma, which manifests itself on the written page.

While different, each book chronicles life events, seemingly autobiographical—one set in childhood and the other in full adulthood. Memoir grounds his work, and lyrical leaps transform it into poetry. *Chicopee Spur* uses the Japanese haibun form, which consists of a prose poem plus a haiku. The 17th-century poet Basho developed the genre as he traveled. Ortolani uses haibun to good effect, as he logs a journey through time. Repeated themes include mortality, weather, mental weather (depression) and nature. The poet is a suburban dweller who looks for natural cycles on city streets and in blackberry thatches. The book reads like a daybook with regular, if not daily, entries.

The haiku for the prose poems in *Chicopee Spur* are invariably good, like this: "deepening / the night between blackberries," and this, "blackbird—releasing / in cattail." Both show an interesting inversion. The negative space between the blackberries focuses on the qualities of darkness in both night and the color black. In the other, the cattail releases the blackbird, rather than the bird taking flight. The prose backstory for these two quick-cutting haiku (and

a third) amplify the power of both prose and poem. "My daughters
and I pick blackberries in the shadows," as the prose poem opens,
"the July night coming on hot and heavy as a canvas awning." Into
this scene comes a vagrant man who passes them in the thicket
and nods. Two days later, his obituary appears in the news, which
reveals that the man had died just after he passed the poet. Was he
death, itself, or did he simply suffer "misfortune"? This ominous and
mysterious title poem, placed second in the volume, sets up the tone
of the entire book.

Ortolani does not write a repetitious stack of uniform haibun.
He varies individual haiku to conform to the spirit of the form—
with its koan-like twists—rather than a strict syllable count.
Readers enter his dramas and share the poignant moments. The
book's content centers on concerns of a middle-aged person, as
elderly parents sicken and die. This coincides with the teenage
children's trajectory away from their birth families in another kind of
abandonment. This double loss creates an autumnal mood exactly
right for haibun.

One of my favorites, "At the Trading Post Bridge," begins: "A
dozen cranes stand in the floodwaters. They are as stoic as statues.
Eighteen wheelers roar down the road." The prose poem continues
to describe the whiz of traffic, country-music radio, wind, and a jake
brake. The poem that caps the scene is this: "in the bridge shadow /
a beer bottle / polished to stone." Ortolani works with stasis and
movement, with nature and human activities.

*How Wally Lost His Thumb and the Boy Scouts Became
Cannibals: New and Selected Poems* begins with childhood memories
and spans, chronologically, the development of this Charlie Brown
character who might resemble the author's imagination of himself,
or his counterpart. The extended adolescence of a man-child
character allows for rebellions. In the acknowledgements for the
book, Ortolani writes:

As the Wally collection grew, I decided early on to include them
in whatever chronological collection of poems they fit into. . . .
In putting this *New & Selected* collection together, I gathered
many of the poems that fit Wally's story, changing where need

be the occasional name or detail that helped the series congeal
as a single piece.

So this is a long-term project, now bound as a single book, with
years between the start and finish. This life-long sequence reads like
one long poem.

The opening poem, "Crayon Sucker," is set in kindergarten with
the character Wally as a class clown, established and confirmed at
the end during a parent-teacher conference:

> His parents learned to accept Cs
> from their above average,
> crayon sucking child.

The third-person narration gives the poet distance from the
story-poems, so this is a fictional biography, rather than an
autobiographical piece. Like William Trowbridge's poetic biographies,
The Complete Book of Kong and the Fool archetype in *Ship of Fool*, the
vignettes fit together to create a mosaic picture. Each poem stands
alone, but together the sum of parts is a *tour de force*.

The sequence of childhood to teenage years is rich with
anecdotes, such as in "Wally and the Cowboys Drive Across Low
Water Bridge in High Water." Boys in an old Ford crossing a flooded
bridge survive their bad choice, but at a cost, as they "breathed for the
first time / all week." Wally's puppy love is a set-up for comedic lyrics.

Wally serves as an alter ego to the poems' narrator, the bad
twin who double dates with him and terrifies everyone with reckless
driving ("Double Dating with Wally"). Some of the poems are from
the narrator's own viewpoint. "Roseland Road House," written after
a failed bar fight, addresses Wally and laments, "I wish you had
followed me / into the parking lot, and explained."

The adult stories about Wally continue the saga of a
marginalized nonconformist. In "The Day Wally Was Murdered Love
Poem," the attack situation becomes humorous, as the lover's knife
turns out to be plastic. Yet there is an edge, "She insisted / he had /
no heart." The short-lined form is bladelike on the page, and it also

moves quickly, like the knife assault. Ortolani shows, throughout the book, his skill as a poet, as content fits into apt forms.

The story of Wally reflects the story of many like him who live in the Little Balkans area of southeast Kansas. The book celebrates the rebel Wally as it documents a regional history that recedes into the past. Wally is sighted singing a hymn in a cave, in "Wally Sings Amazing Grace in an Arkansas Cave." Then, in "Wally Smokes a Cigar with Sam Clemens," the last poem of the book, he says, "Wally disappeared shortly after buying his first smart / phone." The narrator fills in some details about a move north to Minnesota after trading his Ford truck for a houseboat. This last act was preparation for reenacting Huck Finn's travels on the Mississippi. The tie-in to this maverick of United States literary history ends the book with a familiar yet unresolved conclusion. As usual, Ortolani uses his allusions well here. This book is a sustained reflection on memory, life's arc, community, and friendship.

THOMAS E. KENNEDY (LEFT), A *NEW LETTERS* REGULAR, AT THE 2008 NATIONAL MAGAZINE AWARDS, LINCOLN CENTER, NYC, WITH ROBERT STEWART (RIGHT). *NEW LETTERS* WON FOR KENNEDY'S ESSAY "I AM JOE'S PROSTATE." PHOTOGRAPH BY STEVE FRIEDMAN.

Poems of Ruthless Empathy

By Marilyn McCabe

Book Review:

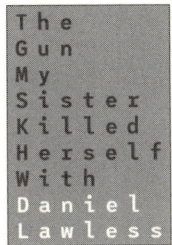

> *The Gun My Sister Killed Herself With,*
> by Daniel Lawless, Salmon Poetry, 2018.

With such a ruthless title, author Daniel Lawless assures us that the poems within have no holds barred. These uncompromising poems are filled with life's tough events, and Lawless' phlegmatic voice narrates it with wryness and wit, but also empathy.

In these poems, people fall into holes; struck bodies lie in the street; there is cancer, schizophrenia, abuse. There are screams and a choir of wig mannequins conducted by a wild man. Through poems that seem to mine his own family history, and also what he views around him with his watchful eyes, Lawless is exploring ". . . the bruise / That bloomed beneath the bruise / And the one beneath that one" (from "Velda the Seer"). The empathy of those lines keeps this collection from being as dark as it should be, given the subjects and imagery.

Sonically the poems are glorious mouthfulls, from the chewy Latin of a Catholic upbringing to tightly wound, alliteratively unfolding narratives. His wordplay is inspired and inspiring: A bright flock of birds taking off is a "shriekshape." A dolphin has "pleathered flesh." A crabby father's hand-rolled cigarettes are "half-bents." A spouse insists on "spendy-taxiing" to a destination. Of a first kiss from a young, would-be Egyptologist: "Her thin tongue slithered into my mouth like a dry hieroglyph."

Sound adds a savagery to some of these poems of merciless memory: In "View from a Treehouse," the narrator watches his schizophrenic brother being led away:

> Bobby and I fumbling limp Marlboros in mittens
> While we watched through the spy-slot

We'd sawed with a steak knife into a gap
Between two sheets of plywood spiked with nails . . .

The poem moves from the almost comical Bs and Ms of some kind of silly innocence, to the Ss and the hard Ks of what they saw and how disturbing: this brother become a stranger going, going, gone, as the car drives him away. "Your fifteen-year-old face freckled / In the window with sleet, fat and pale. . . ."

Comedy also threads through the book, from two elegies to dead squirrels—well, more confessions of low moments in the narrator's childhood career, really, to the sprawling and unruly similes of "Down in the Mangroves," where:

There's a pink condom and a hairweave
Like symbols in a Renaissance painting,
And one of those red rubber coin purses
Like the mouth on Señor Wences' hand.

An example of the great humanity of these poems is "In the Alzheimer's Ward at Saint Jude's." The narrator finds himself acutely uncomfortable in the titular location, and staring into a fish tank: "A tiny wreck and treasure chest, the yellow ape / In cast iron boots I take to be my alternate / In uselessness. . . ."

The fish mirror the mute and unreachable occupants of the ward, with whom he can communicate no more effectively than his tapping on the tank walls. Then the poem, itself, if not the narrator, turns to face the ward and wrap its confused residents in its arms:

All those bright echoing rooms
Where nameless children play or ghostly tulips bloom,
A green squawking stalks its perch
Above a grand odd-shaped thing.

The Gun My Sister Killed Herself With is full of such capacious moments; Lawless' poems embrace the world with its pocks and scabs.

To Own the World

By Allison Field Bell

Book Review:

> *Marrying Kind*, by K.L. Cook,
> Ice Cube Press, 2019.

K. L. Cook's new collection, *Marrying Kind,* builds a world of stories that connect and overlap, contrast and unsettle. It is a multi-generational book, with some stories displaying a multitude of voices: fathers and sons, daughters and mothers, wives and husbands. For Cook, marriage exists as a condition of lovers, families, colleagues, professions, canines. It is an act of devotion, one that is lodged in the human spirit. From a teenage boy discovering Shakespeare for the first time to a long-married woman coping with the loss of her husband, Cook's characters are complex and nuanced, reminding us of what it is to love.

What is so compelling about *Marrying Kind* is the lens through which Cook forces the reader to examine a character's actions. In the story "Barbarians," the narrator watches a drama of irreparable proportions unfold before her. The reader experiences characters collide with or embrace the confines of their lives. A young boy is helpless in the face of his mother's impending and life-altering conflict with his stepfather. A prematurely grieving husband turns away from his former fiancé and their child and then makes the same mistake with his dying wife. "I am already on the road," he says, "a one-way street, heading away." The collection blurs the lines between what devastates us and what keeps us whole.

In *Marrying Kind*, place exists not just as the setting of a honeymoon, or the exotic refuge from a former life, or a stroll through campus, but with real stakes in the world of story. With landscapes ranging from Las Vegas to Florida to West Virginia, Cook invites the reader to imagine place as a defining extension of character. A married couple tries their luck and their love in Vegas.

An economically devastated professor battles a fish on the Florida Coast. A dean experiences place as a psychological movement from the high desert of Arizona to the cold and green country of West Virginia.

Marrying Kind also enters into a particular conversation about masculinity and how it influences relationships. For Cook, masculinity is as complex and nuanced as our current political atmosphere, including the pressures of male relationships with women, male egos, their careers, and the places they inhabit.

Ultimately, through his stories, Cook reveals what is universal about the human experience: the intellectual passions, the shape-shifting natures of families and couples, the hope-filled prospects of a future just beyond the horizon. As one of Cook's characters puts it, "I want us to move in the world like we own it." *Marrying Kind* is an elegant portrayal of that yearning, one that leaves the reader filled with empathy and self-reflection, the great feat of all worthwhile fiction.

–SUPPORT–

The Environmental Defense Fund
Solve environmental problems https://www.edf.org/

Green America
Seek a sustainable society https://www.greenamerica.org/

National Resources Defense Council
Become an activist https://www.nrdc.org/

Political Action
Write, call, or visit your senators, reps, governor.

Recalibrating Voices from the Triangle Shirtwaist Fire

By AnnaLee Barclay

Book Review:

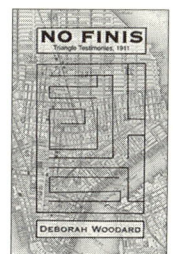

> *No Finis: Triangle Testimonies, 1911,*
> by Deborah Woodward, Raveena Press, 2018.

I have not thought about New York City's Triangle Shirtwaist Factory fire of 1911 since middle school. The story is horrific, and I remember imagining myself just a few years older, working long hours in cramped, dirty conditions for little pay, only to face the choice of being engulfed by flames or jumping to my death: excruciating pain or a few seconds of freedom before instantaneous nothing. I remember my child mind linking that choice to 9/11, which happened when I was in my first-grade classroom on Long Island. My father picked up my brother and me from school early, and at home we watched clips on the news of people who jumped from offices in the twin towers. Bodies fell like birds that forgot how to fly. While the memories of September 11th have remained vivid for me—close in proximity to our house at the time—the Triangle Fire had not entered my thoughts until this extraordinary and nonconventional poetry collection by Deborah Woodard.

Woodard presents us with a few pages of summary as to the events of the fire, including excerpts of eye-witness accounts. "The fire galvanized New York, but it was unique only in scale," we're reminded, and that numerous other tragedies existed among a largely poor class of immigrants. This brief history lesson is followed by poems that Woodard constructed using the transcripts from the trial of *The People of New York v. Isaac Harris and Max Blanck* (co-owners of the Triangle Factory). The dialogue between the factory's lawyer and each witness has been cut, cropped, manipulated, and is devoid of any identification as to who is talking:

You were just straightening out the first body bag?

I was.

Did Officer Lauth make a mark?

He marked how the girl's head was turned birdlike to one side.

————

I gave a blind man a dime for her outside the Regal

> —From "Mr. Steuer and Floyd Mance, Fireman,
> Hook and Ladder 20"

While at times, one easily can tell when the lawyer is speaking versus the witness, these stand-alone lines require you, as a reader, to imagine who is speaking. One witness account titled "Mr. Steuer and Ethel Monick" continues for two pages and then has a break line, similar to the above excerpt, followed by, "I want to buy a music box, and then a phonograph." I imagined that the witness, presumably a young immigrant girl, whispered this to herself after she was asked to step down from the witness stand. The nature of both visual and literary collage includes disorientation and removal of context, and so Woodard manipulates text to give the reader an opportunity to use his or her imagination.

Illustrations by John Burgess throughout the book depict the Triangle factory and its fire. One of his black-and-white drawings looks, upon first glance, simply like a maze. It is captioned, "Put your finger on the diagram where the opening was." The notes tell us that this is a drawing of the ninth floor of the building, the deathtrap floor. It's easy to assume that in the actual transcript, Mr. Steuer was merely asking a witness to point out something on a different photo, a piece of evidence in the courtroom. This illustration follows one of Woodard's poems, a particularly brutal round of questioning that ends:

Any bodies found on the roof?

No, sir.

Any bodies found on the fire escape?

No, it had buckled early on.

And the record of the deceased was made by Officer Lauth?

I am not sure.

That will be all.

————————

We tried to keep their hats and purses with them

> —From "Mr. Steuer and Andrew Ott, Fireman,
> Hook and Ladder 20"

By combining Woodard's skill at placing lines from the primary source with Burgess' simple, yet startling diagrams, the reader is left with a gut-punch of desperation and hopelessness, which the girls in the maze of tables and walls on the 9th floor must have felt.

No Finis: Triangle Testimonies, 1911 moves quickly, but the impact is startling. The tragedy was born from serious negligence, but the factory owners had a lawyer who was as unrelenting as the flames. Rather than focusing on the disappointing outcome of the trial, these poems and illustrations, that were clearly constructed with a tender hand and heart, depict the individual human lives that were taken or undeniably altered by the Triangle fire. In this collection, Woodward shows how collage poetry can get to the heart of tragedy· what happens when vulnerable people are exploited, how language can change outcomes, and how human minds can carry a story inside every moment, even when context is stripped away.

THE ROBERT DAY AWARD FOR FICTION
ENDOWMENT-FUND CAMPAIGN

We invite you to help us achieve our goal of a $200,000 endowment to sustain the Robert Day Award for Fiction. It takes a sizable financial commitment to discover, reward, and promote great, new writing in this way. This fund offers a $2,500.00 first prize for the best short fiction, chosen from entrants anywhere in the world. We have an annual mid-May deadline.

The people listed below have made it possible for us to establish the award, as we continue to work toward our endowment goal. Contact the *New Letters* office if you are able to provide tax-deductible support for this effort. On behalf of the Day family, we thank those who have donated so far.

donors up to $15,000
Jeff and Mary Haynes Weinberg (pledge)   Marjorie E. White
Walton and Deborah Beacham

donors up to $1,000
Elizabeth Broun   Mary Anne Dolan

donors up to $500
Phyllis Springer Sipahioglu   Fred Whitehead
John Milnes Baker

donors up to $100
Gretchen and Bill Gillen   Joseph L. Holt   James F. Hoy
S. Wesley Jackson   Denise Low   Bonita M. Oliva

* * *

Donate via the SUPPORT button at the upper right of our website, www.newletters.org, or contact us at 5101 Rockhill Road, University of Missouri-Kansas City, Kansas City, Mo. 64110.
New Letters: (816) 235-1169, newletters@umkc.edu.

New Audio Programs
New Letters on the Air

New Letters on the Air features more than 1,000 half-hour audio interviews and readings by many of the greatest poets, fiction writers, essayists, and playwrights of the past 40 years. The weekly series and its archives can be heard four ways:

- On public-radio stations across the country. Call your public-radio program director for information.
- Via free weekly podcast (see *www.newletters.org/on-the-air* for subscription information).
- Streamed weekly on our website.
- On CD for $7.99 or audio download for $3.99. Browse our catalogue at *www.newletters.org*.

For more information about the program, contact the host and producer, Angela Elam, or assistant producer, Jamie Walsh, toll-free at (888) 548-2477, or email radio@newletters.org. *New Letters on the Air* has recently broadcast the following shows:

Kansas Poets
Laureate, Part I
August 2019.

Kansas Poets
Laureate, Part II
September 2019.

Jo McDougall
September 2019.

Xánath Caraza,
Part I
April 2019.*

Sergio Troncoso
September 2019.

Mia Leonin &
Gustavo Adolfo Aybar
September 2019.

Xánath Caraza,
Part II
September 2019.*

Laura Kasischke,
Part I
September 2019.

Randall Freisinger,
Part I
September 2019.*

Laura Kasischke,
Part II
October 2019.*

Alan Proctor
November 2019.*

Meg Wolitzer
November 2019.*

Stewart O'Nan
November 2019.

Bojan Louis
November 2019.

Randall Freisinger,
Part II
December 2019.*

December Festivals
December 2019.*

Cheers to All
the Years
December 2019.*

Premier Broadcast *

Video about *New Letters on the Air,*
www.newletters.org

VISITORS LOG:
THE *NEW LETTERS* GUEST BOOK

Univeristy of Missouri-Kansas City Cockefair Chair Writer-in-Residence **Ben Lerner** joined Angela Elam, producer and host of *New Letters on the Air*, for a public interview on Oct. 3rd; screenwriter **Kevin Willmott** spoke with Editor-in-Chief Robert Stewart before his interview with UMKC professor Mitch Bryan at a Writers for Readers event on Nov. 13th; poet

Alice Friman and her husband, Bruce, had dinner with Robert Stewart and others on Nov. 16th; *New Letters* Writer-in-Residence Whitney Terrell interviewed writer and editor **John Freeman** for a Writers at Work round table at the Kansas City Public Library on Nov. 19th; Angela Elam interviewed prose writer **Ron Currie Jr.** on Nov. 19th at the Johnson County Public Library.

Honor Roll
The 2019 *New Letters* Literary Awards

Final Judges for 2019: Kevin Wilson (fiction),
Gary Dop (poetry), Sheila Kohler (essay)

RUNNERS UP & HONORABLE MENTIONS

Rebecca McKanna, fiction
Kristen Beachy, fiction
Meg Todd, fiction
Emily Ransdell, poetry
Lazar Trubman, essay

FINALISTS IN FICTION

Francisco González   Diana Amsterdam   Holly Menino
Charlie Watts   M. Haile Summerfield   Philip Golabuk
Elaine Wang   Jennifer Chianese   Amanda Jackson
Michael Knoedler   Paul Byall   Brian Crawford   Reena Shah

FINALISTS IN POETRY

Deborah Bogen   Ryan Bonner   Roger Craik
Patricia Farewell   Diane Glancy   Vernita Hall
W.J. Herbert   Jen Karetnick   Christopher Kempf
Karen Kovacik   Orlando Menes   Susie Meserve
Nancy Miller Gomez   Lucy Ricciardi   Soren Stockman
Therese Tappouni   Cynthia White

FINALISTS IN THE ESSAY

Laura Jean Baker   Chad Davidson   Maurice Labi   Carol Clouse
Jodie Noel Vinson   Kristin Owens   Sandy Robertson
Erik Gleibermann   Jessica Burdg   Gina Evers   John Price
Laura Distelheim   Candice Kail

CELEBRATIONS
NEWS FROM OUR AUTHORS & ARTISTS

Stephen Dunn's poem "Nothing Will Warn You," from *New Letters* vol. 85 nos. 2&3, will appear in his collection *Pagan Virtues*, due out from W.W. Norton & Co. in 2020; **Albert Goldbarth**'s poems "I'm tired of my student Scott Galloway," from *New Letters* vol. 80 no. 1, "This Bookmark," from *New Letters* vol. 80 nos. 3&4, "Album" and "Switch," from *New Letters* vol. 83 nos. 2&3, and "Rhapsody at the End of Human Language," from *New Letters* vol. 84 no. 4, appear in his collection *The Now* (U of Pittsburg P, 2019); **Dion O'Reilly**'s poem "Alaska," from *New Letters* vol. 52 no. 4, appeared on *Verse Daily* on Nov. 8th; **Gary Young**'s series of prose poems, from *New Letters* vol. 52 no. 4, appeared on *Verse Daily* on Nov. 7th.

(CIRCA 1943, CLUB FRONTENAC, DETROIT.) LEFT TO RIGHT: ARDATH JUNE BETTS, ROY WINGROVE DAWES, SALLY RAND (BURLESQUE, OSTRICH-FEATHER FAN DANCER, NATIVE OF ELKTON, MISSOURI, HICKORY COUNTY), WITH OTHER FRIENDS.

NOTES ON CONTRIBUTORS

DEBORAH BACHARACH is the author of *After I Stop Lying* (Cherry Grove Collections, 2015). She is an editor, teacher, and tutor living in Seattle, Washington.

PETER BALAKIAN is the author of seven books of poems, most recently *Ozone Journal* (U of Chicago P, 2015), which won the 2016 Pulitzer Prize. He teaches at Colgate University and lives in Hamilton, New York. (A *New Letters on the Air* author.)

ANNALEE BARCLAY is a photographer and writer from Long Island, New York.

CYNTHIA BEARD is a freelance photographer and assistant managing editor at BkMk Press. She lives in Prairie Village, Kansas.

ALLISON FIELD BELL is a writer from Sebastopol, California.

JANET BURROWAY's *Writing Fiction: A Guide to Narrative Craft* (10th edition) is the most widely used creative-writing text in America, and her multi-genre *Imaginative Writing* is out in a fourth edition. Her most recent novel is *Bridge of Sand* (Houghton Mifflin, 2009; Hopcyn P, London, 2013) and her memoir *Losing Tim* was published in 2014 (Think Piece Publishers). She was awarded the Florida Humanities Council's 2014 Lifetime Achievement Award in Writing and is Robert O. Lawton Distinguished Professor Emerita of the Florida State University. She and her husband, Peter Ruppert, divide their time between Wisconsin and Chicago. (A *New Letters on the Air* author.)

CARL DENNIS is the author of 13 books of poetry, including *Practical Gods* (2001), *New and Selected Poems (1974–2004)*, *Callings* (2010), and *Night School* (2018). A winner of the Pulitzer Prize and the Ruth Lilly Prize, he taught in the English department of the State University of New York and in the Warren Wilson Writing Program in North Carolina. He lives in Buffalo, New York.

MARIE ÉTIENNE is the author of 11 books of poems and nine books of prose. In 2009 her book *Roi des cent cavaliers* was translated into English as *King of a Hundred Horseman* and won the PEN Award for Poetry in translation. She lives in Paris, France.

GLORIA BAKER FEINSTEIN is a fine-art photographer, originally from Kentucky and now based in Portland, Oregon. Her work has been featured in this magazine many times; she, herself, has been making pictures for over 60 years.

BRIANNA FLAVIN is an assistant professor of English at the University of Northwestern in St. Paul, Minnesota.

DIANE GLANCY is the recipient of a Minnesota Book Award, an American Book Award, and the 2014 Lifetime Achievement Award from the Wordcraft Circle of Native Writers. Her most recent poetry collections are *The Book of Bearings* (Wipf and Stock, 2019) and *It Was Over There by That Place* (Atlas Review, 2019). *Island of the Innocent: a Consideration of the Book of Job*, is forthcoming from Turtle Point Press in 2020. She lives in Shawnee Mission, Kansas. (A *New Letters on the Air* author.)

ALBERT GOLDBARTH's collections of poetry have twice won the National Book Critics Circle Award. His most recent collection is *The Now* (U of Pittsburgh P, 2019). He has been reading and appearing in *New Letters*, he says, longer than some of you have been alive. He lives in Wichita, Kansas. (A *New Letters on the Air* author.)

DONNA GORDON was a 2016 finalist for the *New Letters* Prize in Fiction. She is the recipient of a Stegner Fellowship and a PEN Discovery Award, among others. She was a 2017 Tennessee Williams Scholar at the Sewanee Writers Conference and a fellow at the Vermont Studio Center in 2017 and 2018. She lives in Cambridge, Massachusetts.

CARYN MIKKIAM-GOLDBERG served as the poet laureate of Kansas from 2009–2013. She is the author of two dozen books, including *Miriam's Well*, a novel (Ice Cube P, 2018); *Everyday Magic: A Field Guide to the Mundane and Miraculous* (Meadowlark, 2017), and *Following the Curve*, poetry (Spartan P, 2017). Founder of Transformative Language Arts concentration at Goddard College, she leads writing workshops widely. She lives in Lawrence, Kansas. (A *New Letters on the Air* author.)

MARILYN HACKER won the National Book Award and the PEN/Voelcker Award for Poetry, and is the recipient of fellowships from the National Endowment for the Arts and the Guggenheim Foundations. She is the author of 13 books of poetry, including *A Stranger's Mirror: New and Selected Poems 1994-2003* (W. W. Norton). She is a translator of Arabic and Francophone poets. She lives in Paris, France. (A *New Letters on the Air* author.)

MICHAEL HENSON is the author of four books of fiction and four collections of poetry and has worked as an addiction counselor and community organizer. He is a co-editor of *Pine Mountain Sand & Gravel*, the annual publication of the Southern Appalachian Writers Cooperative. He lives in Cincinnati, Ohio.

RICHARD JONES is the author of 16 books of poetry, including *Stranger on Earth* (Copper Canyon P, 2018). Editor since 1980 of the literary journal *Poetry East*, he curates its many anthologies, such as *Paris*, *The Last Believer in Words*, and *Bliss*. In 2020 he will publish his 100th issue. He is a professor of English at DePaul University in Chicago, where he directs the creative writing program.

GEORGE KALAMARAS is the author of 15 collections of poetry, eight of which are full-length, including *Kingdom of Throat-Stuck Luck*, the winner of the Elixir Press Poetry Prize (2011), and *The Theory and Function of Mangoes* (2000), the winner of the Four Way Books Intro Series. His most recent collection of poetry is *The Hermit's Way of Being Human* (CW Books, 2015). He is professor of English at Purdue University, Fort Wayne, Indiana.

KAREN KOVACIK, poet laureate of Indiana from 2012–2014, is the author of several poetry collections *Metropolis Burning* (Cleveland State, 2005), *Beyond the Velvet Curtain* (Kent State U P, 1999), and *Nixon and I* (Kent State U P, 1998). Her most recent translations include *Scattering the Dark* (White Pine, 2016), an anthology of Polish women poets, and Jacek Dehnel's *Aperture* (Zephyr, 2018), a finalist for the 2019 PEN Award for Poetry in Translation. She is a professor of English at Indiana University–Purdue University, Indianapolis.

ANGIE SIJUN LOU is a Kundiman Fellow from Seattle and Shanghai. She teaches creative writing at the University of California-Santa Cruz.

DENISE LOW, Kansas poet laureate 2007–2009, is winner of the Red Mountain Press' Editor's Choice Award for her poetry collection *Shadow Light*. Her memoir *The Turtle's Beating Heart: One Family's Story of Lanape Survival* (U of Nebraska P) was a finalist for the Hefner Heitz Kansas Book Award. She recently relocated to Sonoma County, California. (A *New Letters on the Air* author.)

TERRANCE MANNING JR. is a graduate of Purdue University's M.F.A. program in creative writing. His essays have won *Narrative* magazine's spring 2017 story contest, the 2017 *Iowa Review* award for nonfiction, and the *Crazyhorse* nonfiction prize. He lives in Pittsburg, Pennsylvania.

MARILYN MCCABE's work has garnered her an Orlando Poetry Prize, the Hilary Tham Capital Collection award, and two artist grants from New York State Council on the Arts. She lives in Saratoga Springs, New York.

JOHN MOESSNER was a Writer-for-Readers Fellow for Literacy KC, an organization that employs creative writing graduate students at the University of Missouri-Kansas City to teach writing to teens and adults enrolled in Literacy KC classes. He serves on the board of directors for The Writers Place and lives in Kansas City, Missouri.

REBECCA OFIESH is a visual artist and writer living in Kansas City, Missouri. With advanced studies in fine art and humanities, she uses the camera to explore the nature of light, vision and perception. She has been exhibiting with The Kansas City Society for Contemporary Photography since 2016.

H.C. PALMER's first book of poems, *Feet of the Messenger*, was published by BkMk Press in 2017. A retired internist, he works with a military veterans' writing program in partnership with the Kansas City Public Library, The Writers Place and The Moral Injury Association of America. He lives in Lenexa, Kansas. (A *New Letters on the Air* author.)

EMILY RANSDELL was runner-up for the *New Letters'* 2018 and 2019 Patricia Cleary Miller Award for Poetry. She lives in Camas, Washington.

TRISH REEVES is the recipient of fellowships from the National Endowment for the Arts, Yaddo, and the Kansas Arts Commission. Her latest book of poetry, *God, Maybe*, was published in 2018 by Scattering Skies Press. She leads Johnson County Kansas Corrections' Changing Lives Through Literature seminars, and is a Kansas humanities scholar in literature. A professor of English at Haskell Indian Nations University for 21 years, she is retired and lives in Prairie Village, Kansas. (A *New Letters on the Air* author.)

ELI REICHMAN began his photojournalism career at *The Los Angeles Times* in 1978. A 1982 recipient of the Pulitzer Prize, Reichman has also worked at *National Geographic, The Kansas City Star* and *The Tulsa Tribune*. Born and raised in south Kansas City, Reichman now resides in Charlottesville, Virginia, working as a filmmaker and documentarian.

GERALD STERN received the National Book Award for poetry in 1998 for *This Time: New and Selected Poems* (W. W. Norton, 1999) and was named as a finalist in 1991 for the Pulitzer Prize in poetry for *Leaving Another Kingdom: Selected Poems* (HarperCollins, 1990). He is the recipient of a Ruth Lilly Poetry Prize, and the Wallace Stevens Award from the Academy of American Poets, among others, and was appointed as New Jersey's first poet laureate in 2000. His most recent collections of poetry include *Blessed as We Were: Late Selected and New Poems* (W. W. Norton, 2020). He lives in New York, New York. (A *New Letters on the Air* author.)

WILLIAM TROWBRIDGE's seventh poetry collection, *Vanishing Point*, was published by Red Hen Press in April, 2017. His eighth, an expanded collection of poems featured in the graphic chapbook *Oldguy: Superhero* (Red Hen P, 2016), was published in 2019. He is a faculty mentor in the University of Nebraska-Omaha's low-residency M.F.A. in Writing Program and was poet laureate of Missouri from 2012 to 2016. He lives in Lee's Summit, Missouri.

CAROL ZASTOUPIL is an artist whose paintings appear in numerous private and public collections. A veteran teacher and museum educator, she lives in Kansas City.

---

* *New Letters on the Air* authors" have featured readings and interviews on the half-hour radio series *New Letters on the Air*. For CDs or audio downloads of those programs, contact us at (816) 235-1159, radio@newletters.org, or visit www.newletters.org.

Winner of the G. S. Sharat Chandra Prize for Short Fiction,
Selected by Stewart O'Nan

Stone Skimmers

Jennifer Wisner Kelly

In beautifully lucid prose, Jennifer Wisner Kelly explores the separate
fates of friends from Old Stonington, Connecticut, at home and out
in the world, as they and those around them wrestle with death and
abandonment, secrets and betrayals, and the complicated bonds of
families and friendships.

—Sarah Stone

BkMk Press
University of Missouri-Kansas City • www.umkc.edu/bkmk